INTERACTIONS II
A Speaking Activities Book

INTERACTIONS II
A Speaking Activities Book

Deborah Poole
San Diego State University

Emily Austin Thrush
Memphis State University

McGraw-Hill, Inc.

New York   St. Louis   San Francisco   Auckland   Bogotá   Caracas
Hamburg   Lisbon   London   Madrid   Mexico   Milan
Montreal   New Delhi   Paris   San Juan
São Paulo   Singapore   Sydney   Tokyo   Toronto

This is an ⌐EBI⌐ book

Interactions II: A Speaking Activities Book

3   4   5   6   7   8   9   0

ISBN   0-07-553807-5

Manufactured in the United States of America

Text design and production: Donna Davis
Cover design: Cheryl Carrington
Cover illustration: František Kupka; *Lines, Planes, Depth,* c. 1920–22.
Oil on canvas, 31½″ × 28½″, Albright-Knox Art Gallery, Buffalo, New
York. Charles Clifton and George B. and Jenny R. Mathews Funds, 1977.
Drawings: Eva Mautner

Grateful acknowledgement is given to Sally Gati for all photographs
with the exception of the following:

page 55, bottom left, Mary Gill; 56, Andrew Sachs/Black Star;
76, 77, 78, 79, Los Angeles County Museum of Art; 82, courtesy NASA.

CONTENTS

PREFACE

INTERACTIONS: THE PROGRAM

INTERACTIONS consists of ten texts plus two instructor's manuals for in-college or college-bound nonnative English students. INTERACTIONS I is for high-beginning or low-intermediate students, while INTERACTIONS II is for low-intermediate to intermediate students. Within each level, I and II, the books are carefully coordinated by theme, vocabulary, grammar structure, and, where possible, language functions. A chapter in one book corresponds to and reinforces material taught in the same chapter of the other books at that level for a truly integrated, four-skills approach.

Each level, I and II, consists of five books plus an instructor's manual. In addition to the speaking activities books, they include:

A Communicative Grammar I, II: Organized around grammatical topics, these books include notional/functional material where appropriate. They present all grammar in context and contain a wide variety of communicative activities.

A Reading Skills Book I, II: The selections in these books are written by the authors and carefully graded in level of difficulty and amount of vocabulary. They include many vocabulary-building exercises and emphasize reading strategies, such as skimming, scanning, guessing meaning from context, understanding the structure and organization of a selection, increasing reading speed, and interpreting the author's point of view.

A Writing Process Book I, II: These books use a process approach to writing, including many exercises on pre-writing and revision. Exercises build skills in exploring and organizing ideas, developing vocabulary, using correct form and mechanics, using coherent structure, editing, revising, and using feedback to create a final draft.

A Listening/Speaking Skills Book I, II: These books use lively, natural language from a variety of contexts—dialogues, interviews, lectures, and announcements. Listening strategies emphasized include summarizing main ideas, making inferences, and listening for stressed words, reductions, and intonation. A cassette tape program with instructor's key accompanies each text.

Instructor's Manual I, II: These manuals provide instructions and guidelines for use of the books separately or in any combination to form a program.

The grammatical focus for the twelve chapters of INTERACTIONS II is as follows:

1. review of basic verb tenses

2. nouns, pronouns, adjectives, and articles

3. modal auxiliaries and related structures

4. the present perfect with *still, yet,* etc.; *would/used to, was/were going to;* the past perfect tense

5. phrasal verbs and related structures

6. coordinating conjunctions; clauses of time, condition, reason, contrast, and purpose; the future perfect tense

7. transitions; the past perfect continuous tense; clauses of time

8. clauses and phrases of comparison

9. the passive voice

10. adjective clauses

11. common uses of infinitives and gerunds

12. *wish, hope,* and imaginative conditional sentences

INTERACTIONS II: A SPEAKING ACTIVITIES BOOK

Rationale

INTERACTIONS II: A SPEAKING ACTIVITIES BOOK is designed to give students the opportunity to practice their speaking and listening skills and develop fluency in English. Although some of the activities encourage the use of specific grammar structures, in general the activities are intended to promote fluency and improve communication skills.

Many of the activities involve problem solving. These help students develop skills in negotiation, reducing miscommunications, and using various levels of directness and indirectness that are impossible to teach in more formal ways.

Most of the activities are designed to be performed in small groups or pairs to make the communication as "natural" as possible. Small-group work also ensures that each student will have the greatest opportunity for participation.

Many of the activities are task-oriented, so that the students focus their attention on a task rather than on language. This allows for more natural, less self-conscious communication and keeps motivation and interest high, since students know they must complete the task within a certain amount of time.

Chapter Organization

The text consists of twelve chapters, each of which has a central theme. The themes correspond to those in the other books of the INTERACTIONS program. The activities in the chapters are of varying lengths and may take from fifteen to twenty minutes of class time up to several hours on successive days. There are both short and long activities in each chapter, so the instructor may choose those that fit his or her lesson plan.

Teaching Hints

As language teachers, most of us are struggling to continually shift more attention and responsibility from ourselves to our students. For many, the advantages of group or pair activities as a way of centering class attention on students have become more and more obvious. With group or pair activities, the instructor is free to help those who need extra attention, the spirit and dynamic of the class is greatly enhanced, students get constant rather than occasional practice, shy students seem to blossom, and students feel more comfortable asking questions as they sense that the instructor is more available. In spite of these and numerous other advantages, many questions persist among even very experienced instructors regarding both procedural and pedagogical aspects of using group or pair activities. The following questions represent some of those most often asked:

1. How will the class see your role? How do you make students feel they are not being abandoned or left to "teach themselves"? These are possibly the most crucial questions to consider when using group and pair activities in your classes. It could be very easy to put students in groups and simply let them go about a task on their own. The most important (but sometimes most difficult) thing to do is make sure the class knows you are available, interested in whether and how the students complete the task, and convinced of its value. Usually it is helpful if you move about the room from group to group. You may want to interrupt, simply listen in on what is happening, or become a participant in the activity. Generally, however, if you are positioned in such a way that the students know you are available, they will feel freer to pose questions regarding the activity, vocabulary, grammar, etc. Your presence in this manner and their perception of you as available and willing to help them will go a long way towards alleviating any feelings they have of not being "taught."

   During a group activity your role changes from that of an instructor to a facilitator or information source. In order to ensure that the students feel comfortable, several things must always take place:

   a. Clear and strict time limits must be set. This is a way of letting the students know you are still directing and controlling what is going on even though you are not in front of them in the usual role. Students know that they must try to complete the task within a specific time period. This usually encourages more efficient work on their part.

b. The directions must be absolutely clear. The students should have no questions about what they are supposed to do while working with others. This may, of course, require explicit demonstration on your part.

c. The students need to understand why they are being asked to do a specific exercise. It is often beneficial to explain the purpose of an activity before you begin it.

2. What about the noise level and the movement of the chairs? Students soon become accustomed to both and almost expect to be moving their chairs in order to form groups to work with other students. For many, also, the noise level provides them with a sense of security because not everyone is listening to them speak English, so that they become more willing to take risks when speaking.

3. How often do you use group activities? Use them as often as you want to and feel they are productive. The frequency should depend on the class and on you as the instructor. As a rule, all group work needs to be followed up with a meeting of the class as a whole where groups report in some way on what took place. Most of the activities in this book that involve group or pair work can be adapted for use by the class as a whole. We would encourage you to use group work only to the extent that you feel it is beneficial to the class.

Beyond the Classroom

INTERACTIONS II: A SPEAKING ACTIVITIES BOOK is designed to take maximum advantage of the English-speaking environment outside of class. Numerous activities involving interviews, phone conversations, newspapers, and field trips are included. We believe that drawing on the out-of-class environment will make the language acquisition process more rapid and the students more comfortable as they become involved in the communities where they reside.

We hope that those instructors in non-English-speaking countries will take full advantage of the English resources that are available. English newspapers; American, British, Canadian, or Australian companies or high schools, and English-speaking tourists or residents are all resources that can be effectively tapped for use by your students. Taking advantage of these resources will expose your students to many contexts of natural language use that cannot be duplicated inside the classroom, and we would encourage any adaptation of our activities that would make this feasible.

Acknowledgements

The authors would like to acknowledge the invaluable assistance of Mary McVey Gill of EBI and the inspiration and creativity of James W. Hale, Susan Firestone, Rosemarie Goodrum, C. A. Johnston, Wendy Newstetter, Irving Penso, Mark Tanner, Richard Young, and many talented teachers at both ELS Atlanta and USC's American Language Institute. Thanks also to Anne Weinberger of Random House for her work on the production of the book.

D.P.K.

E.A.T.

1 EDUCATION AND STUDENT LIFE

GETTING TO KNOW YOUR CLASSMATES

You are going to ask a classmate some questions to get to know him or her.

1. Work in pairs.

2. Ask your partner questions to find out about each of the categories in the chart that follows.

Example: residence:

>   Where did you live five years ago?
>   Where will you be living a year from now?
> achievements:
>   What is something you achieved last year?
>   What do you hope to achieve five years from now?

3. Take notes on your partner's answers in the chart.

4. Your partner will also interview you and take notes on your answers.

5. After you have finished, find a new partner. Tell your new partner as much as you can about your first partner.

	five years ago	last year	this year	a year from now	five years from now
residence					
school					
work					
marriage					
children					
hobbies					
problems					
achievements					

DISCUSSING EDUCATION IN THE UNITED STATES AND CANADA: WHAT DO YOU THINK?

You are going to share your ideas about American education with your classmates.

1. Form a circle with all the students in your class. The instructor will sit outside the circle, listening to your discussion.

2. With your classmates, discuss what you think the answers to the following questions are. It is not necessary to write anything.

3. After the discussion, your instructor will tell you his or her answers to the questions.

Questions

1. In the United States and Canada, what's the difference between a *college* and a *university?* What are *community colleges?* For what reasons do some people choose to go to a community college?

2. What is adult education? What is vocational education (vo-tech)? What kinds of classes can you take in adult education programs? Why do people take these classes?

3. What are the requirements to enter an adult education program? A vo-tech program?

4. What is the name of the test most Americans and some Canadians take in order to enter college?

5. When do American or Canadian college students usually begin studying in their major field?

6. What do they study before beginning their majors?

7. Do you think most American college students live in dormitories or apartments or with their families?

8. Do college and university professors usually lecture by giving the same information that is in the text, or do they give different information?

9. When you attend a college or university, when is it appropriate to visit a professor?

10. Which of these English skills do you think a foreign student needs most in college: listening, speaking, reading, or writing? Rank them in order of importance.

11. In North American education, a lot of emphasis is put on extracurricular activities—that is, things students do outside class, such as club activities, athletics, volunteer work, and so on. Why do you think this is? Is this true in your country?

12. Do you think college instructors expect students to ask questions and contribute to class discussions?

OBSERVING A COLLEGE CLASS

Your instructor will make arrangements for you to visit a college class and make some observations. If possible, small groups of students should visit different classes.

1. Go to a college or university class in your community. During the visit, try to answer the questions in the list that follows.

2. After the visit, form groups of three students each and compare your answers to the questions. How were the classes alike? How were they different?

3. Report to the whole class one or two things that you thought were unusual about the class you observed.

Questions

1. How many students are in the class? _____

2. How do late students enter? _____

3. Where are the students when class begins? _____

4. What do they do while the professor is talking? _____

   _____

5. How many students are taking notes? _____

6. Is the class a lecture or discussion? _____

7. How are the chairs arranged—in a circle, in straight rows, etc.? _____

   _____

8. Do students ask questions during the class or wait until the end? _____

   _____

9. What do students do when they have a question but the professor is talking?

   _____

10. How do the professor and students address one another? _____

    _____

11. Are students looking at a book at any time during the class? _____

    _____

12. Does the instructor expect students to speak or answer questions during the class?

    _____

13. Do some students ask questions after class? _____

PARTICIPATING IN A PANEL DISCUSSION: HOW EDUCATION IS CHANGING

You are going to have a panel discussion on how education is changing.

1. Choose three or four students in the class to be on the panel. If possible, these students should be from different countries.

2. The panel will discuss each of the questions that follow. As the discussion proceeds, take notes on what the participants say in the spaces provided.

3. After the panel discusses each question fully, the listeners should say whether they agree or disagree.

Questions

Question 1: Are younger teachers in your country less formal and strict than older teachers? Explain the differences.

Notes: _____

_____

_____

_____

_____

_____

_____

_____

_____

_____

_____

_____

_____

_____

Question 2: Is the philosophy of education changing among the teachers in your country? For example, do you notice a different teaching style among some teachers?

Notes: _____

_____

_____

_____

_____

_____

_____
_____
_____
_____
_____
_____
_____
_____

Question 3: What do you think are the advantages of a more formal educational system? What are the disadvantages?

Notes: _____
_____
_____
_____
_____
_____
_____
_____
_____
_____
_____
_____

Question 4: If you were a teacher, would you want a formal or informal atmosphere in your class? Explain your answer.

Notes: _____
_____
_____
_____

_____

_____

_____

_____

_____

_____

_____

_____

_____

_____

_____

_____

Question 5: Do you have anything like community colleges, adult education, or vocational education courses in your country? What purpose(s) do they serve?

Notes: _____

_____

_____

_____

_____

_____

_____

_____

_____

_____

_____

_____

_____

_____

FINDING OUT ABOUT COLLEGES

1. Look at the items in the list that follows. How important is it to have information about each item before you start college in the United States or Canada?

2. For each item, circle 1 (very important), 2 (important), or 3 (not important).

3. For each of the items you marked "very important" or "important," write the name of a place where you can get this information (a college catalogue, college students, an admissions officer, and so on). Use a separate sheet of paper.

Information about . . .	very important	important	not important
1. how to apply	1	2	3
2. how to register	1	2	3
3. English language requirements	1	2	3
4. English classes for foreign students at the university	1	2	3
5. kinds of tests given	1	2	3
6. the role of the academic advisor	1	2	3
7. the role of the foreign student advisor	1	2	3
8. the use of the library	1	2	3
9. recreational facilities on the campus	1	2	3
10. the grading system	1	2	3
11. course requirements for your major	1	2	3
12. student/teacher relationships	1	2	3
13. the amount of help to expect from teachers and other students	1	2	3
14. rules concerning classroom behavior	1	2	3
15. types of papers students must write	1	2	3

Follow-up

1. Have one student put the numbers of the items on the chalkboard (1–15). Count the number of students who thought each item was important or very important and

put the total beside the item number. Which are the most important items to most of the students in the class? Which are the least important?

2. Choose five of the most important items. Discuss where to get the information on those items.

3. Divide into five groups. Each group will be responsible for getting some general information on one of the items (some of the answers will be different for different colleges). Try to find out about a local college or a college that someone in the class is planning to attend.

SOLVING CLASSROOM PROBLEMS: WHAT WOULD YOU DO?

You are going to decide what to do in one of the following college classroom situations.

1. Form four groups. Each group should take one of the four situations that follow.

2. The members of each group should read the situation and then discuss the questions that follow it.

3. Each group should choose one member to report to the class. This person should summarize the situation and the group's answers to the discussion questions.

Situation 1

Mrs. Fitch teaches Western civilization at a community college. Three of her students do not like her class. They think she talks too fast, doesn't answer questions from the students, and doesn't explain clearly how she wants them to write their papers. The three students decided to talk to Mr. Neston, a history professor that they like very much. They told Mr. Neston about Mrs. Fitch and why they don't like her. Mr. Neston asked if they had told Mrs. Fitch about their problem with her class. They said no, they couldn't possibly do that. Mr. Neston likes these students and believes they are telling the truth. He talks to Mrs. Fitch and tells her what the students said. Mrs. Fitch is very unhappy. She doesn't understand why the students didn't talk to her about the problem. She is also a little angry with Mr. Neston.

Discussion Questions

1. Who do you think students should talk to when they have a complaint about a class (the teacher, another teacher, the head of the department, or someone else)?

2. What do you think Mr. Neston should have done in this situation?

3. If you were Mrs. Fitch, what would you do now?

Situation 2

Tomohiro, a Japanese student, is in Mr. Erickson's American history class. Many times, Mr. Erickson has called on Tomohiro to answer a question about the reading assignment in class, but Tomohiro never answers. One day Mr. Erickson decides to talk to Tomohiro about this problem. Mr. Erickson says, "Tomo, I'm very concerned about your work in this class. You never seem to be able to answer the questions, and I have to assume from that that you haven't read the assignments. Now, unless you start doing your assignments at home and participating in class, I'm afraid you're not going to get a very good grade in this class." Tomohiro replies, "Yes, sir. I will try."

In fact, Tomohiro has been reading the assignments and knows all the answers. However, he feels that Mr. Erickson is not allowing enough time for a student to answer a question before he goes on to the next student. This is a cultural misunderstanding. A study has shown that the maximum amount of time allowed in an American class for a student to begin answering a question is seven seconds. In a Japanese class, the average amount of time is much longer. Japanese teachers expect students to think about the answer first, then speak.

Discussion Questions

1. What mistake did Mr. Erickson make?

2. If you were Tomohiro, what would you do?

3. Have you experienced any cultural differences like this in any of your classes?

Situation 3

Carlos and Abdullah have a good friend from Canada named Jack. All three of them are taking Psychology 101 this semester. This morning, Jack came to class a few minutes late. The professor was already talking. Jack came into the room quietly, sat down, and started taking notes. After class, Carlos said to Abdullah, "I don't think Jack likes us anymore. He didn't even say hello this morning. Let's just have lunch without him."

Jack sees his friends leave for lunch and is very unhappy that they don't ask him to join them. He doesn't understand why they are angry.

Discussion Questions

1. Why does Carlos think Jack doesn't like them?

2. Why didn't Jack say hello when he came to class?

3. If you were Jack, would you have said hello?

4. If you were Carlos or Abdullah, would you be angry at Jack?

Situation 4

A small community college recently held its final exams. During one exam, the instructor saw a student looking at a paper on her desk. She also saw the student sitting next to her looking at the same paper. When this happened, the instructor took both students' papers and told the students that they could not finish the exam. Later, the dean of students talked to them and told them that they could either take an F for the course or leave the school. The students protested that they had not been cheating, but only "looking." One of them decided to leave the school and the other decided to take an F for the course.

Discussion Questions

1. Do you think the teacher acted in a fair or appropriate way? If not, what should she have done?

2. What might the dean of students have done differently?

3. Do you think this situation might really happen? In what kind of school?

2
CITY LIFE

DECIDING WHAT IS MOST IMPORTANT IN A HOME

What's most important to you about where you live?

1. Rank the list of items that follow from 1 to 14. Give a 1 to the most important, 14 to the least important. Do this individually.

_____ being able to walk to a grocery store or market

_____ having one bedroom for each person or couple

_____ having a yard

_____ having appliances (dishwasher, washing machine, dryer)

_____ being on the ground floor, so there are no stairs to climb

_____ being able to have parties or play loud music without bothering your neighbors

_____ having a quiet atmosphere, with no loud noise from neighbors

_____ not having to do outside work (for example, yard work or painting)

_____ knowing people who live near you

_____ owning the property where you live

_____ living in an area where there is not much crime

_____ living close to where you work or go to school

_____ living near relatives or very close friends

_____ having recreational facilities (swimming pool, tennis courts, etc.)

2. Discuss the results with your class. Which items were the most important to the most people? Which were the least important?

CHOOSING BETWEEN SMALL TOWNS AND BIG CITIES

You are going to discuss the advantages and disadvantages of small towns and big cities.

1. Form groups of three to five students.

2. In the chart that follows, list the advantages and disadvantages of living in small towns; then list the advantages and disadvantages of living in big cities. Each person in the group should write the same list.

3. Find a partner from another group. Discuss and compare your answers.

4. With the whole class, discuss whether you would prefer to live in a small town or a big city. Give your reasons.

Small Town
Advantages: _____

_____

_____

_____

_____

_____

_____

Disadvantages: _____

_____

_____

_____

_____

_____

_____

Big City
Advantages: _____

_____

_____

_____

_____

_____

_____

Disadvantages: _____

_____

_____

_____

_____

_____

_____

_____

PUTTING A STORY IN ORDER:
"THE RECKLESS DRIVER"

"The Reckless Driver" is a story about Tom, a reckless city driver, and what happened to him one morning on the way to school. The map on the next page shows the area where he was driving. The paragraphs that follow tell the whole story. The story is not in order, however. Your task will be to put it in order.

1. Divide into groups of seven students. (Seven is the ideal number. If there are fewer than seven in one group, some students can take more than one part.)

2. Each student should choose one of the paragraphs in the story. You will be responsible for that paragraph only.

3. Read your paragraph and make sure you understand it. Then draw on the map (on the next page) the part of Tom's route that your paragraph describes.

4. Read your paragraph again and make sure you know the information well enough to explain it without looking at the book.

5. When you are ready to explain your part of the story, fold your book back so that only the map is showing.

6. You will have fifteen minutes to:
   a. listen to each person in your group tell his or her part of the story;
   b. decide what the correct order of the story is;
   c. draw Tom's complete route on the map.

Story

A. He was in a hurry, so he drove a little faster until he reached Briarwood Road, where he made a right turn. He got behind a very slow car, so he passed it even though he was in a no-passing zone.

B. In a few seconds he saw a flashing blue light in his rear-view mirror. A policeman gave him a ticket for going through a red light and for reckless driving. Then Tom drove slowly and carefully on to Carlton.

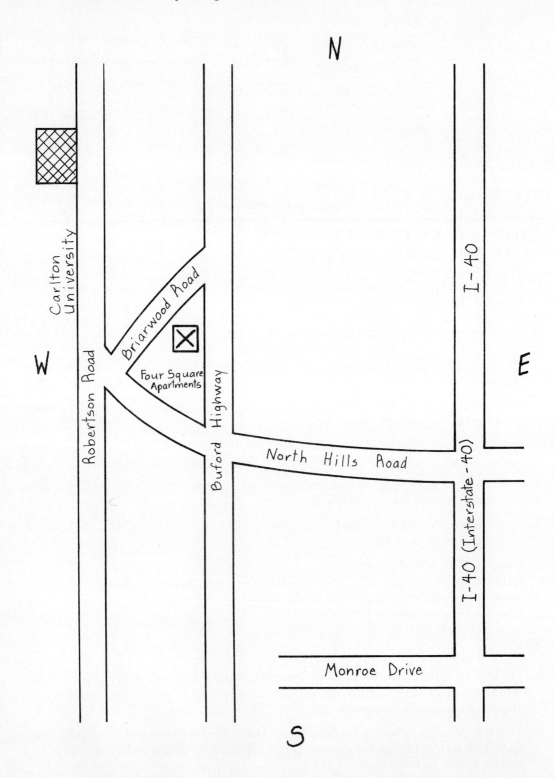

C. Tom began his usual trip to Carlton University by getting on Interstate 40 (I-40), a large highway, at Monroe Drive. He drove north, driving in the left lane most of the way and passing quite a few cars. He was speeding—going about 70 miles per hour although the speed limit was 55 miles per hour.

D. After passing Buford Highway, he had to merge with another lane of traffic, so he speeded up and passed two cars as he continued on his way. Suddenly he remembered that he was supposed to pick up his friend Carlos at the Four Square Apartments.

E. When he reached North Hills Road he made a quick right turn without signaling or stopping. Right after that, when he got to Robertson Road, he saw that the light was yellow, so he accelerated. However, by the time he went through the light, it was red.

F. When he reached the apartments he turned in and honked the horn. Carlos came out immediately and hopped in the car. Tom drove back to Briarwood Road and turned left. He accelerated to about 50 miles per hour, even though it was a 35 miles per hour zone.

G. He got off the expressway at the North Hills Road exit and made a left turn at the traffic light. On North Hills Road he became impatient because the traffic was quite heavy. When he reached Buford Highway, he ran through a yellow light.

GETTING AROUND THE CITY: READING A MAP AND GIVING DIRECTIONS

You and a partner are going to take turns giving directions to get from one place to another in the city of Detroit, Michigan.

1. Look at the map of Detroit on the next page. Student 1 should give directions to get from Grand Circus Park to the Renaissance Center (these two places are both marked 1 on the map). Student 2 should draw on the map, following the directions Student 1 gives. If Student 2 does not finish at the Renaissance Center, then Student 1 should start again at Grand Circus Park and give directions.

2. Next, Student 2 should give directions to get from the Detroit Institute of Technology to the Detroit-Windsor Tunnel (both marked 2 on the map). Student 1 should draw the route on the map.

3. Take turns giving and following directions. Give directions for the following places:
   a. from the bus terminal to the YMCA (3 on the map)
   b. from Detroit Memorial Hospital to Woodward Mall (4 on the map)

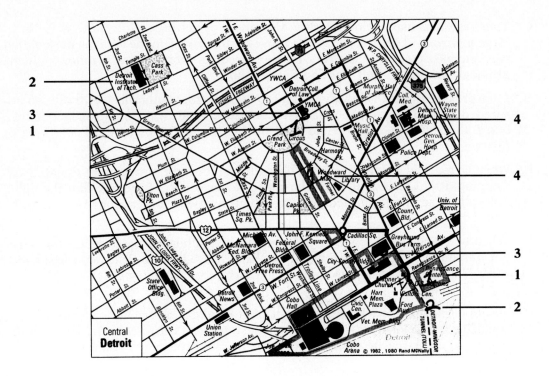

GETTING AROUND THE CITY: TELEPHONE ROLE-PLAY

It is often necessary to give directions over the telephone. It is important to be able to give exact street names and numbers and specific information on where to turn. This exercise will help you practice giving directions in the city where you are living and understanding directions others give you.

1. Work with a partner. Sit back to back (that is, not facing each other). Student 1 should give directions from the school to his or her house or apartment. Give specific street names or numbers. Student 2 should take notes on the directions Student 1 gives. Student 2 should then repeat the directions to Student 1. If Student 2 cannot repeat the exact directions, start over again.

2. Change roles. Student 2 should tell Student 1 how to get to Student 2's house. Student 1 will take notes and relate the directions back.

3. Change partners. Take turns giving directions and relating back directions from school to the following places:
   a. an amusement park

b. a shopping center
c. a beach, lake, or river
d. the airport
e. a museum
f. a sport stadium

Change partners for each new place.

3
BUSINESS
AND MONEY

DISCUSSING MONEY AND BANKING

You are going to share your knowledge of money and banking with your classmates.

1. Form a circle with all the students in your class. The instructor will sit outside the circle, listening to your discussion.

2. With your classmates, discuss what you think the answers to the following questions are. It is not necessary to write them down.

3. After the discussion, the instructor will tell you his or her answers to the questions.

Questions

1. What is a *credit card?*

2. What are the names of the "major" credit cards?

3. What do you need in order to write a check in a store (besides a checkbook and pen)?

4. In what kinds of places can you pay with a check?

5. How can you get cash when the banks are closed?

6. What's the difference between a checking account and savings account?

7. When you use a checking account, how does the bank pay the people to whom you owe money? What is the process by which the money goes from you to the people you pay?

8. In this country, how much cash do people usually carry with them?

CHOOSING THE BEST CHECKING ACCOUNT

Following is some information about five different checking accounts from three different banks. You are going to consider all the accounts and decide which would be best for you.

1. Divide into five groups of one to four students each. Each group should be responsible for one of the types of accounts that follow.

2. In your group, read the information about the account. Ask your instructor if you have questions. Prepare to present the information about your account to the class. Use this "Account Information" chart to help you prepare your presentation.

3. Make a three-minute oral presentation to the class; give all the important information about your account.

4. Take notes while listening to the information about all five accounts. Use the chart on page 25. Then decide which one would be best for you. Tell the class which one you chose and why.

Account Information

1. Name of bank: _____

2. Name of account: _____

3. Minimum opening deposit: _____

4. Service charge: _____

5. Average daily balance to avoid service charge: _____

6. Interest (Note: Some accounts may not pay interest.): _____

7. Additional benefits or special features: _____

_____

Checking Accounts

NATIONAL SECURITY BANK

Regular Checking Account

This account gives you the convenience of a personal checking account *and* the benefit of an interest-earning savings account.

□ Annual interest is $5\frac{1}{4}$%.

□ Interest is compounded monthly.

□ Minimum opening deposit is $200.

□ No monthly service charge with an average monthly balance of $1,500.

□ Free checking (no service charge) for senior citizens (over 60).

□ Balance below $1,500, pay 25¢ per check. No monthly service charge.

Super Checking Account

Take advantage of unlimited checking and high money-market interest rates with National Security's Super Checking Account.

□ $2,500 minimum opening deposit.

□ Varying interest rates—currently $6\frac{1}{4}$%.

□ $5\frac{1}{4}$% interest when balance falls below $2,500.

□ Unlimited free checking.

□ Balance below $1,500 for more than 60 days, account changes to regular checking account.

BANK OF TODAY

Regular Checking Account

Open a Regular Checking Account at the Bank of Today with $100 (minimum opening deposit). The service charge varies with your balance and the number of debits against your account (see the chart below). If you keep an average daily balance of $1,000 or more, you won't pay a monthly service charge.

Average daily balance	Service charge	Charge per check	Charge per electronic transaction
$1,000 or more	No charge	No charge	No charge
$500–599	$2/month	20¢	15¢
Under $500	$3/month	20¢	15¢

Interest Checking

Earn $5\frac{1}{4}$% interest with Interest Checking from Bank of Today. The usual minimum opening deposit is $500.

Service charge: There is no monthly service charge when you keep an average daily balance of $2,000. If your average daily balance falls below $2,000, the charge will be $4.00 per month plus 20¢ per check and 15¢ per electronic transaction.

Interest: Your interest will be compounded daily. That means each day you will receive $\frac{1}{365}$ of the annual rate.

   If your balance is zero or less than zero at the end of a statement period, you will receive no interest for that period.

THE STATE BANK

All-in-One Account

The All-in-One Account is the State Bank's complete package of convenient banking services.

  With a minumum monthly balance of $900 or an average daily balance of $1,500, you get all of the following benefits.

□ *Unlimited Check Writing*

  No charge per check—write as many checks as you want.

□ *Personalized checks*

  Order your checks **free**. We have a variety of colors and designs.

□ *Money Orders and Travelers Checks*

  Free whenever you need them.

□ *Annual Credit on a Safe Deposit Box*

  Receive a $15 annual credit toward any size Safe Deposit Box.

All of these benefits with the *All-in-One Account—*

   Minimum monthly balance—$900

        OR

   Average monthly balance of $1,500

        OR

   A $6.00 per month service charge

        OR

   62 and over—no service charge

Open your All-in-One Account with only $500 minimum opening deposit.

| | NATIONAL SECURITY BANK | | BANK OF TODAY | | THE STATE BANK |
	Regular	Super	Regular	Interest	All-in-One
Minimum opening deposit					
Service charge					
Interest Yes/no Amount					
Average daily balance to avoid service charge					
Additional benefits/ special features					

ROLE-PLAYING A FAMILY INHERITANCE

Imagine that an uncle has died and left your family ten thousand dollars ($10,000). Now your family must decide what to do with the money.

1. Work in groups of five. Each person should take one of the roles that follow.

2. Have a "family discussion." Present the point of view of the family member whose role you choose. The family as a group then decides what to do with the money.

3. One person in your group should report the decision to the class. Tell what the group decided to do with the money and why.

Roles

Father: You want to buy a new car. Your old car is in very bad shape, and you have to drive a long way to work each day.

Mother: You want to save the money. You are worried about how the family will live when your husband retires from work.

Grandmother or grandfather: You want the family to add a new room onto the house for you. Right now you are sharing a bedroom with one of the children.

Son: You want to go to France, study French, and go to a university in Paris. Ten thousand dollars would be just enough money to pay for your living expenses for four years.

Daughter: You think the whole family should take a vacation and travel around Europe this summer. It would be educational and enjoyable for everyone in the family.

PUTTING A STORY IN ORDER: "THOMAS HOFFMAN'S EXPENDITURES"

"Thomas Hoffman's Expenditures" is a story about a day in the life of a young man, including all the expenses that he had that day. The paragraphs that follow tell the whole story. The story is not in order, however. Your task will be to put it in order and to figure out exactly how much money Thomas Hoffman spent.

1. Divide into groups of six students each. Each student in the group should be responsible for one of the following paragraphs. (If your group has fewer than six members, some students should take two paragraphs.)

2. Read only your paragraph. Don't read the paragraphs of the other students. As you read your paragraph, fill in the appropriate places in the chart following the paragraphs. The chart has room for you to write down all the money Thomas spent and what he spent it on. Be sure to put the items in the appropriate category.

3. Reread your paragraph as many times as necessary to be able to remember and explain the information to the other students without looking at the book.

4. Look at the expenditure chart on the next page.

5. Your group will have fifteen minutes to do the following:
   a. explain the information in your paragraphs to each other;
   b. decide what the correct order of the story is;
   c. figure out exactly how much money Thomas spent last Friday.

6. Choose one person from your group to report the information to the class. He or she should tell the class what your group thinks the order of the story is and how much you think Thomas actually spent.

Story

A. Later that evening, Thomas met some friends for dinner. Everyone paid individually; Thomas' own meal cost $11, including tax and tip. They then decided to go to a movie, which cost $5.50. When he finally got home, he realized that he had almost no cash left. He was confused by this because he had just gone to the bank that day!

B. Thomas Hoffman woke up late last Friday morning, so he had no time for breakfast. Instead, on the way to work he went to a fast-food restaurant and bought some coffee and doughnuts for a total of $1.85. He also had to stop by the gas station since his car was nearly out of gas. He filled up his tank, which cost $15.25.

C. After a hard morning of work, he went off for a lunch appointment. He met his two colleagues in a restaurant downtown, where he had to pay $2 for parking. They enjoyed a pleasant lunch, including wine and dessert. The bill came to $36.70. Since this was a business lunch, Thomas paid for everyone's meal with his credit card. He also left a tip of $5.75.

D. He then headed home, but on the way he stopped at the grocery store to pick up a few things for breakfast. The bill came to $6.10. Finally at home, he began reading the paper and watching t.v. Someone then knocked on his door and asked him to contribute to the American Cancer Society, so he wrote a check for $25.

E. Back at work, someone asked him to contribute to a gift for one of his fellow employees, who was moving to another city. He gave $5. After answering phone calls and letters for the rest of the afternoon, he left at around 5:00 p.m. He went immediately to the large department store across the street from his office. There he bought a blouse for his sister for her birthday. He charged the gift, which cost $31.98.

F. Before he could go back to work Thomas had a few errands to run. First he went to the post office and bought $5 worth of stamps. He also sent a special-delivery letter for $2.50. Next he drove by the bank to deposit his paycheck and withdraw $75 in cash. Then he dropped by the dry cleaner's. He picked up his clothes, which cost $8.95.

Thomas Hoffman's Expenditures

Category	Amount	Description
Food:	————	————————————————
	————	————————————————
	————	————————————————
	————	————————————————
	————	————————————————
Contributions:	————	————————————————
	————	————————————————
Gifts:	————	————————————————
	————	————————————————
Gas:	————	————————————————
	————	————————————————
Parking:	————	————————————————
	————	————————————————
Movies:	————	————————————————
	————	————————————————
Dry Cleaning:	————	————————————————
	————	————————————————
Postage:	————	————————————————
	————	————————————————
Total:	————	

CALCULATING YOUR OWN EXPENDITURES

How much money did you spend yesterday?

1. In the chart that follows, list all the expenses you had yesterday (if you can remember them all!). Describe each item and list the amount. Provide the names of the categories for the items, as in the chart for Thomas Hoffman's expenditures in the previous exercise.

2. Discuss your expenditures with your classmates. Who spent the most money yesterday? Who spent the least? Did you buy anything that you didn't need?

Category	Amount	Description
Food		
_____	_____	_____
_____	_____	_____
_____	_____	_____
_____	_____	_____
_____	_____	_____
Total	_____	

4
JOBS AND
PROFESSIONS

DISCUSSING WORK HABITS
IN NORTH AMERICA

You are going to share what you know about working customs in North America.

1. Work in groups of three or four students.

2. Try to answer the following questions about jobs in the United States and Canada from what you know or what you think. Take notes about your group's answers.

3. When you have finished, discuss your answers with the class and your instructor.

Questions

1. An employee of a large company is supposed to be at work at 8:00 a.m. How late can he or she be and not get in trouble? _____

   _____

2. What are the normal working hours in most offices? What days do most people have to work? _____

   _____

3. At what time do most workers eat lunch? How long do they have for lunch? _____

   _____

4. How many fifteen-minute breaks do most workers get each day? _____

   _____

5. What are workers supposed to do if they get sick? If they have car trouble? _____

   _____

6. How much vacation time do most office or factory workers get? How many holidays do they get? _____

   _____

7. If workers don't like something about their jobs, who should they talk to: other workers, their immediate supervisor, another manager, or the president of the company? _____

   _____

8. Who determines how much pay workers get? Are there any government regulations about salaries? _____

   _____

RANKING OCCUPATIONAL PRESTIGE

Different occupations have different salaries and responsibilities, and they also have differing degrees of something called "prestige." This is hard to define, but you can think of it as the amount of respect that people in that occupation get from other people. You are going to take a poll to see which occupations have the most prestige in the United States and Canada.

1. Form groups of four or five students. Look at the following chart of occupations. In your group, rank these occupations from 1 to 15. Occupation 1 has the most prestige, and Occupation 15 has the least. Your group must agree on the ranking. Write the numbers in the first column.

2. After you have ranked the occupations, take the chart and interview two or three people from the United States or Canada. Ask them to rank the occupations in the same way. Write the answers in the columns marked "Person 1," "Person 2," etc.

3. Bring your results to class. Compare them with the results that the other students got. Make a list that tells how many number 1 rankings the job got, how many number 2 rankings, and how many number 3 rankings.

4. Answer the following questions about the results:
   a. Were any of the answers in the poll you took different from the answers in your group?
   b. Were any of the results of the poll surprising to you?
   c. Look at the occupations that ranked the highest in the poll you took. What factors seem to determine "prestige" (money, education, power, etc.)?

Occupations	Group ranking	Person 1	Person 2	Person 3
Engineer				
Carpenter				
Governor of a state				
Doctor				
Lawyer				
Dentist				
Nuclear physicist				
Bank manager				

Occupations	Group ranking	Person 1	Person 2	Person 3
College professor				
Chairman of the board of a large corporation				
Owner of a small business				
Professional athlete				
High school teacher				
Television news anchorperson				
Computer programmer				

ROLE-PLAYING A JOB INTERVIEW

Imagine that the government is building a highway outside your city or town. They need to hire four people immediately for the project. These include a flag waver, an engineer, a crane operator, and a supervisor. You are going to role-play job interviews for these people.

1. Choose four people in your class to be interviewers. Each will interview applicants for one position:
   Interviewer 1: flag-waver
   Interviewer 2: engineer
   Interviewer 3: crane operator
   Interviewer 4: supervisor

2. All other students should choose one of the roles from the list of applicants that follows.

3. Try to remember the information for your role.

4. The class should divide into four groups. Each group should have an interviewer and the applicants for that job. The four groups should do the interviews at the same time.

5. After everyone finishes, each interviewer should report to the class. The report should tell who got the job and why the interviewer decided to choose the candidate.

Applicants

Candidates for Flag Waver

1A   *Education:* high school graduate
      Experience: none
      Skills: none
      Note: Needs first job to get experience. Willing to work hard.

2A   *Education:* Tenth grade
      Experience: Worked as flag waver on three other projects. Previous employers say this person's work is okay. Sometimes comes to work late.
      Skills: none

3A   *Education:* high school graduate
      Experience: Worked as a flag waver on a road repair job for two months. Good recommendations from previous employer.

Candidates for Engineer

1B   *Education:* civil engineering degree from Massachusetts Institute of Technology
      Experience: manual labor on construction jobs in summer
      Skills: Operates construction equipment and knows computer programming.

2B   *Education:* high school graduate
      Experience: Twenty years working on road construction. Started with manual labor, but learned from engineers. Designed road system on last two jobs.
      Skills: Operates all equipment for road building.

3B   *Education:* two years engineering school
      Experience: Four years in highway designing. Started as an assistant to engineer; promoted to head engineer on last job.
      Skills: Cannot operate construction equipment.

Candidates for Crane Operator

1C   *Education:* eighth grade graduate
      Experience: Worked on father's farm for ten years. No employment history.
      Skills: Drives a tractor, operates farm machinery.

2C   *Education:* high school graduate
      Experience: Did manual labor (hand digging) on two road projects. Learned to operate a crane on the last one, but was fired for getting into a fight with another worker.
      Skills: can operate a crane

3C   *Education:* high school graduate
      Experience: Some construction work; excellent recommendations.
      Skills: none
      Note: Very intelligent. Needs job to support two children. Can learn quickly.

Candidates for Supervisor

1D   *Education:* high school graduate
      Experience: Two years supervising road repair crews.
      Skills: Good communication skills with workers.

2D   *Education:* college degree in management
      Experience: Managed hamburger restaurant for five years. Good recommendations.
      Skills: None related to highway construction.

3D   *Education:* college degree in urban development
      Experience: Four years supervising highway construction; previous employer says this person had a communication problem with the workers.
      Skills: Has operated most highway construction equipment briefly.

TALKING ABOUT PROFESSIONS

You are going to ask and answer questions about professions.

1. You are going to *be* one of the people in the list of professions that follows. Decide who you want to be.

2. Take turns being in the spotlight. When you are in the spotlight, other students can ask you any questions they choose.

   Example: What is your name?
             How old are you?
             What kind of work do you do?
             Where are you from?
             Could you tell us something about your family?
             How did you learn to _____?
             Tell us about your job.

3. Answer as if you really are in the profession you chose. You know everything about this profession and can answer any question. *Use your imagination!*

Professions

1. architect	9. police officer
2. professional tennis player	10. factory worker
3. rock star	11. t.v. news reporter
4. travel agent	12. piano player
5. airplane pilot	13. astronaut
6. hairdresser	14. dentist
7. photographer	15. restaurant owner
8. taxi driver	

ANALYZING THE CHANGING LABOR FORCE

You are going to complete graphs showing some of the changes in the labor force in various countries.

1. Form groups of four students each. Look at the graphs that follow. Students 1 and 2 will use Graphs 1 and 2; Students 3 and 4 will use Graphs 3 and 4.

2. Students 1 and 2 should place their desks facing each other. Student 1's graph has some of the information about the percentages of the population working in industry in fifteen countries.* Student 2's graph has the rest of the information. Student 1 and Student 2 should ask each other questions and give each other information until they both have all the information in the graphs. Do not look at each other's graphs.

   Example: What percentage of the people in Colombia worked in industry in 1960 (1970)?

3. Students 3 and 4 should do the same thing with Graphs 3 and 4.

4. Following the graphs are some questions. Answer the questions for your graphs.

5. Students 1 and 2 should now tell Students 3 and 4 about their graphs. Don't give all the details but tell about general trends and include information from the questions you answered.

6. Students 3 and 4 should tell Students 1 and 2 about their graphs. Again, focus on general trends.

*Working in industry means working for a company; this does not include farmers, individual owners of small stores, or people who produce something at home to sell (rugs, baskets, clothes, and so forth).

Percentage of Population Working in Industry in Fifteen Countries

The first bar for each country is the figure for 1960;
the second bar is the figure for 1970.

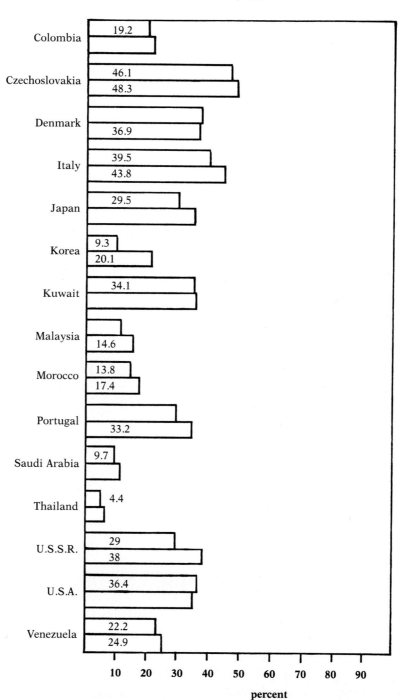

Graph 1

Percentage of Population Working in Industry in Fifteen Countries

*The first bar for each country is the figure for 1960;
the second bar is the figure for 1970.*

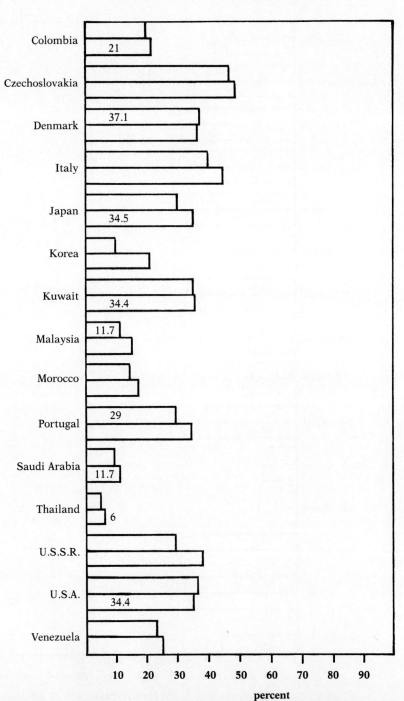

Graph 2

percent

Percentage of Women Working Outside of the Home in Fifteen Countries

*The first bar for each country is the figure for 1960;
the second bar is the figure for 1970.*

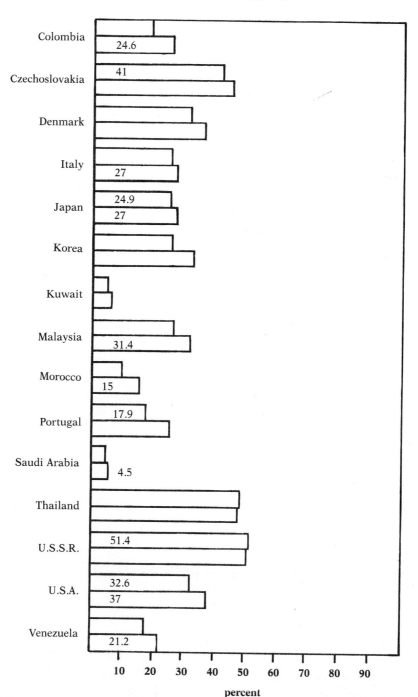

Graph 3

Percentage of Women Working Outside of the Home in Fifteen Countries

The first bar for each country is the figure for 1960;
the second bar is the figure for 1970.

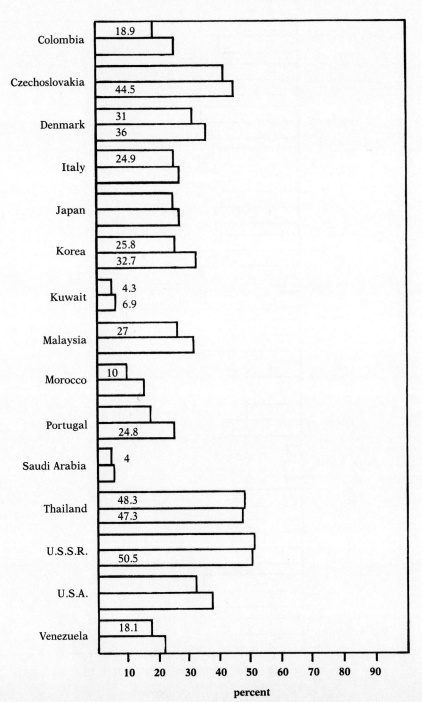

Graph 4

Colombia	18.9
Czechoslovakia	44.5
Denmark	31 / 36
Italy	24.9
Japan	
Korea	25.8 / 32.7
Kuwait	4.3 / 6.9
Malaysia	27
Morocco	10
Portugal	24.8
Saudi Arabia	4
Thailand	48.3 / 47.3
U.S.S.R.	50.5
U.S.A.	
Venezuela	18.1

percent

Questions for Graphs 1 and 2

1. Which country showed the biggest gain in population working in industry from 1960 to 1970?

2. If you are from a country on the graph, what was the increase in population working in industry in your country? Do the figures surprise you? Did you think more or less of the population was working in industry? What do you think the figure might be now?

3. What countries showed a decrease in the percentage of population working in industry from 1960 to 1970? Why do you think the figure decreased? What other kinds of jobs do you think those people are working in now?

Questions for Graphs 3 and 4

1. Which country had the largest increase in the percentage of women working outside of the home? The smallest?

2. If you are from a country on the graph, what was the change in the percentage of women working between 1960 and 1970 in your country? Do the figures surprise you? What do you think the figure is now?

3. What kinds of work do *most* women do in your country?

5
LIFESTYLES

COMPARING LIFESTYLES OF YOUR CLASSMATES

You are going to find out something about the lifestyles of your classmates.

1. Read the following list ("Find the person in the class who . . ."). Stand up and move about the room, asking the questions below.

2. When you find a person who fits one of the descriptions, write his or her name in the blank. Find a person for each description.

Find the person in the class who . . .

1. has the largest family _____

2. spent the most money yesterday _____

3. watched the most t.v. last weekend _____

4. has seen the most movies in the past two weeks _____

5. traveled the farthest last year _____

6. ate the largest breakfast today _____

7. lives the farthest from school _____

8. studied the most last night _____

DISCUSSING THE CHANGING ROLE OF WOMEN

You are going to find out about the role of women in a different culture.

1. Find a person in your class from another country. If possible, find someone from a background very different from yours.

2. Take turns asking each other the following questions. You will have about one-half hour to do this.

3. Take notes on the answers. Then present the information to the class. Summarize the answers briefly; do not read all the questions and answers. Your instructor may ask the class to take notes during the reports and use them to write a composition on women's roles in various countries.

Questionnaire

1. Does your mother have a profession? If so, what does she do? _____

_____

What did she do before she married? Does she ever talk about what she did (or didn't

do)? _____

_____

2. Do you have any sisters? If so, how many? _____
   What are their plans? Do they want to be housewives or do something different?

   _____

   _____

   Are they attending, or planning to attend, a college or university? _____

   _____

   How much freedom do they have to date men or decide on their own careers? Do you

   consider them "liberated women"? _____

   _____

   _____

3. What are the most typical professions for women in your country? Are women
   beginning to work in professions such as medicine, law, and business?

   _____

   _____

   _____

   How do most men in your country view women professionals? _____

   _____

   How would you feel about going to a woman doctor or lawyer? _____

   _____

4. In your country, have there been any demonstrations by women? If so, about what?
   Why? _____

   _____

   If not, do you think there might be demonstrations in the future? _____

   _____

5. Are there any courses in schools in your country that prepare women for careers in
   technology, repair of machines, or construction (such as classes in computer work,

   car repair, or carpentry)? _____

   _____

   _____

6. Do the government and other institutions in your country encourage equality for women? If so, in what ways? _____

_____

7. Do you think that the role of women at home, in society, and at work is changing in your country? If so, how?_____

_____

CONDUCTING A DEBATE: WORKING WOMEN

What is a *debate?* Discuss this with your classmates and instructor.

You are going to conduct a debate on the following topic: "Is it acceptable for women with children between the ages of two and five to work outside the home?"

1. Divide into two equal groups. Group 1 is the group that thinks it *is* acceptable for women with children between the ages of two and five to work outside the home. Group 2 is the group that thinks it *is not* acceptable.

2. In your groups, discuss and list all the possible reasons you can think of in favor of your group's position. Write them in the following spaces. You will have fifteen minutes to do this.

Reasons	**Name**

3. You must have at least one reason (argument) for each group member. Decide who will present each argument. Write each person's name beside the argument he or she will present.

4. Bring your chairs together for the debate. Line up like this:

Group 1   ○ ○ ○ ○ ○ ○ ○ ○ ○ ○
Group 2   ○ ○ ○ ○ ○ ○ ○ ○ ○ ○

5. Here is the format for the debate:
   a. A speaker from Group 1 presents his or her argument. (It may be very short—only a sentence or two.)
   b. Group 2 has approximately five minutes to respond. Anyone from Group 2 may speak during this time. Group 1 members may speak also, but only in response to Group 2.
   c. After no more than five minutes, the cycle begins again. Group 2 presents its first argument briefly. Group 1 may then respond, and Group 2 may answer Group 1. Each student should have a chance to present his or her argument. Then the class as a whole will discuss the debate.

GIVING A SHORT SPEECH

You are going to give a very short speech (two to three minutes in length) on a topic of interest to you.

1. Read the following list of topics. Choose one of them (or choose a topic of your own that concerns "lifestyles"). Be sure no one else chooses the same topic.

2. Take about five minutes to plan your speech. Write down some notes to use when you give the speech. Remember, it should be only about two to three minutes long.

Topics

1. The ideal family size is . . .
2. It is (is not) possible to change careers after age forty.
3. The benefits of living in an extended family are . . . (An extended family is one that includes not only parents and children, but also other relatives, like grandparents, aunts or uncles, etc.)
4. The teenage years are the most . . . of your life.
5. The perfect age is . . .

6. The ideal mother is . . .

7. The ideal father is . . .

8. Arguing in a family is (is not) healthy.

9. The father's role in caring for young children should be . . .

10. Difficulties in a new job may include . . .

11. Divorce can sometimes (never) benefit children.

12. A grandparent's role in child-rearing should be . . .

13. One's job (One's family) should come first.

14. It is (is not) important for a husband and wife with children to have the same religion.

VISITING A RETIREMENT HOME

A retirement home is a home for older people. You are going to visit one of these homes to see what it is like. What do you expect it to be like?

1. Find the names of some retirement homes in your community. Use the yellow pages of your telephone directory.

2. Choose one student from the class to call and try to arrange a visit.

3. Discuss with your instructor when you will go and how you will get there.

4. When you visit the retirement home, you will have the chance to speak individually with one or more of the residents. To prepare for this, you are going to write some questions to ask. Do this in groups of three to four students each. In your group, think of all the questions you might ask the people you are going to speak with. Write them in the spaces on page 48. Each person in the group should write the same questions. Your group should write as many questions as possible in twelve minutes.

5. Choose one person from your group to share the questions with the rest of the class. The rest of the class will listen to your questions, and you will listen to theirs. Add questions to your list as you listen to those of the other groups.

6. After the trip, each student should make a report to the class. Describe the person you spent the most time with. Tell three or four interesting facts about him or her. Discuss with the others your general impressions of the retirement home and its residents. Was it as you expected or different? If it was different, how was it different?

Questions

1. _____
2. _____
3. _____
4. _____
5. _____
6. _____
7. _____
8. _____
9. _____
10. _____
11. _____
12. _____
13. _____
14. _____
15. _____

6
TRAVEL AND TRANSPORTATION

PUTTING A STORY IN ORDER: DESCRIBING MARCO POLO'S TRAVELS

As you probably know, Marco Polo traveled from his home country, Italy, to the Orient. There he met the famous Kublai Khan, who gave him many riches and even a political position. The map on the next page shows where Marco Polo traveled. The paragraphs that follow give information about his trip. This information is not in order. Your task will be to put it in order.

1. Divide into groups of five students each. (Five is the ideal number.)

2. Each of you should choose one of the paragraphs about Marco Polo's voyage. You will be responsible for that paragraph only. (If there are only four in your group, one student can be responsible for two parts of the story.)

3. Read your paragraph and make sure you understand it completely. Then mark on the map (on the next page) the part of Marco Polo's route that your paragraph describes.

4. Read your paragraph again and be sure you know the information well enough to explain it without looking at the book.

5. Using the map to help you, explain your part of the story to the group.

6. Your group will have fifteen minutes to:
   a. listen to each person tell his or her part of the story;
   b. decide what the correct order of the story is;
   c. draw Marco Polo's complete route on the map.

Story

A. While he was in Asia, Marco Polo traveled from Shang-tu down as far south as Pagan (which is now Burma) and back. After that, Polo even became a government official in one Chinese city, Yang-chou.

B. They then sailed up the western coast of India and across the Arabian Sea, returning to the port of Hormuz. They traveled overland, passing through Tabriz, Trebizona, and Constantinople. Finally, they arrived back in Venice in the year 1295. On their journey to China and back they had covered 15,000 miles (24,100 kilometers) and they had been away for twenty-four years!!

C. Marco Polo sailed on his famous voyage to the Orient in 1271. He left with his father and uncle from Venice and went first to Acre, then a port in Palestine. From there they traveled by camel to the Persian port of Hormuz.

D. The Polos finally left China in 1292. They had gone from Yang-chou to a port in southern China. From there they traveled north of Sumatra and then around the southern tip of India.

E. They wanted to sail from Hormuz to China but were not able to find ships that were durable enough there. Thus, they continued traveling by camel across the deserts and mountains of Asia. More than three years after leaving Venice they finally arrived at the palace of Kublai Khan in Shang-tu.

Source: World Book Encyclopedia, 1983.

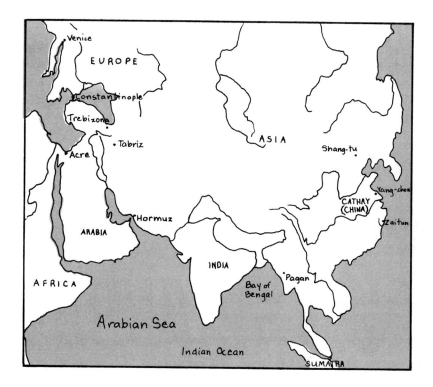

GIVING A TOUR

When you go to a new place, it is often a good idea to take a guided tour. The tour guide tells you a little about the history of the place, present-day activities, and special points of interest. You are going to take the class on a guided tour of a place you are familiar with—but without leaving the classroom!

1. Work in pairs or groups of three.

2. Choose a place, either in the city where you are currently living, in your country, or in a place you have visited. Here are some suggestions:
   a. a capitol building
   b. an amusement park
   c. an unusual phenomenon (for example, the Grand Canyon)
   d. a park
   e. a tourist attraction
   f. a national monument
   g. a shopping center

3. Make notes about the place in the chart that follows.

4. Each person in your group should choose one of the four categories in the chart to talk about. When it is your group's turn, stand up and give your part of the information.

5. Take notes as the other groups give their information. When everyone has finished, your instructor may ask you to say which place you would most like to visit and why.

Tour Information

1. History of the place: _____

_____

_____

2. Current activities there: _____

_____

_____

3. Special points of interest: _____

_____

_____

4. How to get there: _____

_____

_____

Price of admission (if any): _____

Days and hours open: _____

PLANNING A "DREAM VACATION"

You are going to look at some pictures of places to take vacations and think about where you would like to go for a "dream vacation."

1. Look at the photographs of places to go for vacation. Your instructor may bring in some other photos from magazines or travel brochures.

2. Divide into pairs or groups of three. Each pair should choose one of the photos and prepare an oral presentation for the class. In your presentation you should:

a. try to convince the other students that the place you chose would be a good place for a vacation
b. tell about things you can do there
c. tell about things you can see there
d. tell about places you can stay (hotels, cabins, ski huts, tents, and so forth)
e. tell something about the food
f. give a detailed description of the place

Use your imagination.

3. During the other groups' presentations, take notes about what they say about the places they chose.

4. After all the groups have given their presentations, look over your notes. Decide which place you would choose to go to on your "dream vacation." Choose any of the places except the one your group described. Tell which place you chose and why.

1

2

3

4

5

6

7

NORTH AMERICA: THE LAND AND THE PEOPLE

TAKING A POLL: MOVING AND FAMILIES

You are going to interview some North Americans about how often they move and how close they are to their families.

1. Look at the first chart that follows and read the six questions.

2. Interview three North Americans; ask them these questions and take notes on their answers in the spaces in the chart.

3. After the poll, discuss the results with your classmates and instructor. Calculate the average of all persons that the class interviewed for each question and fill out the second chart with this information.

4. Look at the second chart. In your country, how would the answers be different? How would you or your parents answer these questions?

	Person 1	Person 2	Person 3
1. How long have you lived in your present home? In this city?			
2. How many times have you moved in the past fifteen years?			
3. How often do you expect to move in the next ten years?			
4. How far do you live from other members of your family?			
5. How often do you see or talk to your parents?			
6. Have you ever moved away from your family for a job?			

	Average of all persons the class interviewed
1. How long have you lived in your present home? In this city?	
2. How many times have you moved in the past fifteen years?	
3. How often do you expect to move in the next ten years?	

	Average of all persons the class interviewed
4. How far do you live from other members of your family?	
5. How often do you see or talk to your parents?	
6. Have you ever moved away from your family for a job?	

NAMING THE CANADIAN PROVINCES

You are going to look at a map of Canada and learn something about the provinces.

1. Work in pairs and sit facing each other. One student should look at the map of Canada on the next page and one student should look at the following descriptions of the provinces.

2. Together, decide where each province is and write the name in on the correct place on the map.

3. Check your answers with another pair of students.

Provinces

1. Ontario: Ontario has water to the north and water to the south, but it does not touch the ocean.

2. Yukon Territory: Cross the western border of this province and you're in the United States.

3. Nova Scotia: A small strip of land links Nova Scotia to New Brunswick. Halifax is the capital.

4. Alberta: This province is on a plateau just east of the Rocky Mountains.

5. Manitoba: Manitoba borders three Canadian provinces; it also is on a body of water, but not the Atlantic or Pacific Ocean.

6. Newfoundland: This province is part island and part mainland. The island is the easternmost part of Canada, and the mainland part is to the northeast of Quebec.

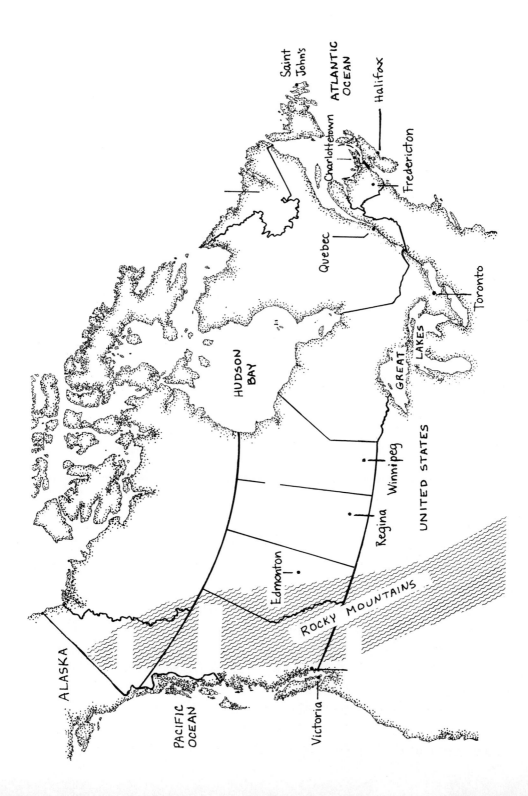

7. Northwest Territories: These have the largest area (and the smallest population) of any of the provinces.

8. New Brunswick: Touching Nova Scotia, this province shares a border with the United States. The capital is Fredericton.

9. British Columbia: This province has a lot of trees and a lot of fish from the Pacific Ocean.

10. Saskatchewan: Saskatchewan is the third province from the West Coast. The capital is Regina.

11. Quebec: This center of French-speaking Canada touches both the Hudson Bay and the Atlantic Ocean.

12. Prince Edward Island: Just a small island, Prince Edward Island is close to both Nova Scotia and New Brunswick. The capital is Charlottetown.

LEARNING ABOUT REGIONS OF THE UNITED STATES

You are going to present information on different regions of the United States.

1. Divide into groups. (Nine groups is the ideal number.)

2. Each group should choose one of the nine regions of the United States that follows. Each group should choose a different region. Outline your region on the map.

3. Study the information on your region.

4. Make a paper sign with the name of your region. Put it on one of the desks.

5. Your instructor will ask questions. There is a list of questions on pages 123–124 to choose from.

   Example: Which area produced the first newspaper?

   Answer the questions about your group. For example, if you are in the New England group, raise your hand.

6. You will get one point for your group if you answer correctly. You will lose one point if you fail to answer or answer incorrectly.

7. After the instructor has asked all the questions, each group should tell the class two or three interesting things about its region.

8. Your instructor may ask you to prepare an oral report on your region.

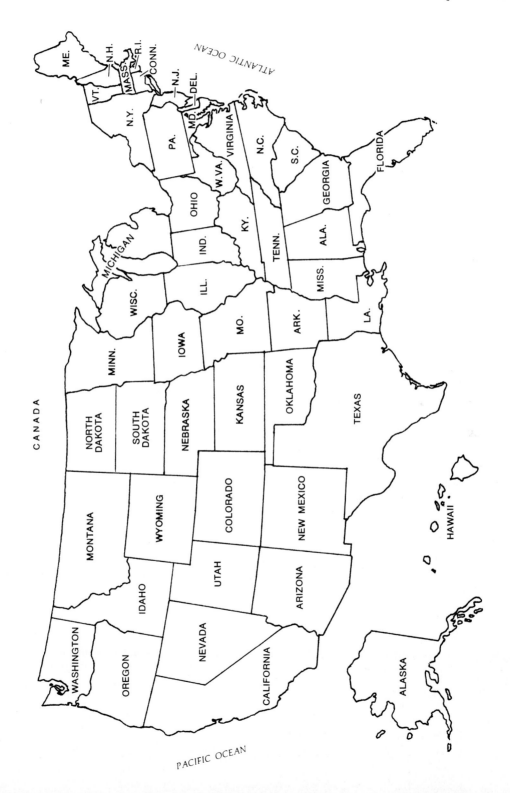

Regions of the United States

Middle Atlantic

New Jersey, New York, Massachusetts

History: 1600: Dutch traders settled the area; then farmers from Denmark, France, Germany, Ireland, and Norway. In 1664 the Dutch surrendered control to the British. Philadelphia was the seat of the Continental Congress, the first government of the colonies. Most of the Revolutionary War against the British was fought in this area. Seat of cultural arts, education, and publishing.

Economy: Commerce, trade, import/export. One-fourth of imported goods coming to the United States come through the port cities of this area. Thirty-two percent of the population works in manufacturing; 2 percent in agriculture. Coal, oil, natural gas, granite, limestone, iron ore.

Geography: Broad coastal area, Appalachian mountains.

Climate: Varies; some extremes of hot and cold for short periods of time.

People: Descendants of Dutch traders and farmers. Mid-1800s: immigration from Italy, Slavic countries, Ireland because of industrialization, availability of jobs. 1840s: immigration from Wales. Mid-1900s: wave of immigration from Eastern Europe (people fleeing from war in Europe). Eighty percent of immigrants to the United States come through these states. 1960s and 1970s: immigration of many Hispanics. Today, one-fifth of all the people in the United States live in this region.

New England

Connecticut, Maine, Massachusetts, New Hampshire, Rhode Island, and Vermont

History: In 1620 Pilgrims and Puritans (strict religious groups) came here from England. Established freedom of religion and freedom of speech. This area played a large part in the American Revolution. Established free education for all. In the 1800s, the first U.S. printing press was here; first newspaper, library, college, public secondary school. Thirteen percent of the country's colleges and universities are in New England, including Harvard, M.I.T., and Yale.

Economy: Early 1800s: agriculture, fishing, shipping. Mid-1800s: traveling merchants sold the products of the new factories. Late 1800s: textiles, leather goods. Present: manufacturing and tourism.

Geography: Long coastal plain, two interior plains, mountains, river valleys.

Climate: Long, cold winters; short, cool summers.

People: Descendants of early British settlers; then in mid-1800s, immigration from other European countries.

Southern States

Alabama, Arkansas, Delaware, Florida, Georgia, Kentucky, Louisiana, Maryland, Mississippi, North Carolina, South Carolina, Tennessee, Virginia, West Virginia

History: Agricultural society before the Civil War in the 1860s. Large cotton plantations. Fought Civil War with northern states because of the attempt of the South to form a new country. Great destruction in the South, where the war took place. The South was very poor for a long time after the war. Industry began to grow in the South because of a good climate and cheap labor costs.

Economy: Before the Civil War, cotton, tobacco, sugar, rice, and other crops were the basis of the economy. Today, there is manufacturing of textiles, furniture, food products, and a large chemical industry. Forestry is also a big industry: the South produces almost all of the country's turpentine and rosins, one-half the wood pulp, paper, and boards, and one-fourth the lumber. The South also has one-third of the country's soft coal and large iron ore deposits. Its farms produce cotton, tobacco, soybeans, corn, rice, sweet potatoes, pecans, peanuts, watermelons, citrus fruits, and sugar.

Geography: Many rivers, rich farmland, forests.

Climate: Mild and humid.

People: All the early settlers in the South came from England, Ireland, or Scotland, with groups of French in Mississippi and Louisiana. Dutch traders brought slaves from Africa to Virginia starting in 1619. Congress stopped the importing of slaves in 1808. No significant foreign immigration from that time until the Cuban immigration into Florida and Georgia in the 1960s and 1970s. One of the fastest growing areas in population in the United States today.

Midwestern States

Illinois, Indiana, Iowa, Kansas, Michigan, Minnesota, Missouri, Nebraska, North Dakota, Ohio, South Dakota, Wisconsin

History: Settled during westward movement from eastern states.

Economy: Mining: richest area in soils and minerals. Minnesota: iron ore; Indiana: limestone; South Dakota: gold; Michigan and Ohio: salt. Manufacturing: production of iron, steel, machinery, paper and rubber products, food products. Farming: corn, wheat, rye, soybeans; raising of cattle, hogs.

Geography: In most states, 80 to 90 percent of the land is farmland. Many grassy plains.

Climate: Cold winters in the northern part; long, hot summers in the southern part.

People: Descendants of early settlers from British settlements. Migration of Scandinavian and Slavic people in mid-1800s. Little recent immigration. This region has a small population for its size. Most of the land is farmland, not big cities.

Southwestern States

Arizona, New Mexico, Oklahoma, Texas

History: Indians settled in this area 25,000 years ago, and there is still a large Indian influence. Peak Indian civilization 1100–1300 A.D. Spanish explorers arrived in the 1500s and 1600s. Founded Santa Fe, New Mexico, in 1610. Starting in the 1800s, westward movement from eastern English settlements. People were looking for gold, animal furs; building railways; herding cattle. From 1846–1848, the United States and Mexico fought for control of this area.

Economy: Cotton, cattle, citrus fruits, copper, oil. Texas has 6 percent of the oil reserves of the world. Tourism due to warm, dry climate.

Geography: Extremes. Mountains, plains, valleys, gorges, deserts.

Climate: Warm and dry. Desert areas hot.

People: Four main cultures: (1) Indian: 285,000 on reservations and throughout the states. Thirty-five percent of the Indian population of the United States lives in this area. (2) Spanish-American: first European settlers; live predominantly in small farming communities. (3) Anglo-American: descendants of people who migrated from the East. (4) Mexican-American: a growing population.

Rocky Mountain States

Colorado, Idaho, Montana, Nevada, Utah, Wyoming

History: Prospectors looking for gold in the 1800s were the first settlers. The United States bought parts of Colorado, Montana, and Wyoming from France in 1803. In 1848 Mexico ceded control of Nevada and Arizona. The United States acquired Idaho in 1846 by treaty with Great Britain.

Economy: Agriculture: cattle, sheep, grains, corn, onions, potatoes, beets. Mining: coal, copper, gold, lead, phosphates, silver, uranium, zinc, oil. Manufacturing: food products, lumber, wood products, nonelectric machinery, furniture. Forests: Christmas trees. Tourism: Tourists visit the Grand Canyon; participate in winter sports.

Geography: Plateaus, Rocky Mountains, plains.

Climate: Varies with altitude; hot, dry desert to cold mountain areas.

People: Moved west from eastern British areas. Mormons settled Utah and developed modern methods of irrigation. Although this region contains one-fourth of the land area of the United States, it is very sparsely populated.

Pacific Coast States

California, Oregon, Washington

History: Portuguese and Spanish explorers in 1600s and 1700s. Spanish missions from 1769. Early 1800s: fur traders from Russia, Great Britain, and United States. These groups disputed control of the area. Treaties between the United States and Great Britain and Mexico settled disputes in 1840s. Between 1840 and 1860 thousands of families came to farm. Gold rush in 1848. Manufacturing developed 1920–50; during this time, the population tripled.

Economy: One-fourth of the people work in manufacturing: transportation equipment (especially airplanes), food products, beverages, electronic equipment, machinery, chemicals. Lumber is also important. Agriculture: most of the fruit and nuts in the United States comes from here; vegetables. Minerals: petroleum, natural gas. Tourists: 6 million every year.

Geography: Mountains, valleys, plains.

Climate: Mild and cool west of the Sierra Nevada Mountains. Dryer, more extreme in the eastern areas.

People: Descendants of American Indian populations, early Spanish settlers, early farmers and gold prospectors, plus recent immigration from the East. Large Oriental population, some descended from those brought in 1800s to build railroads. Recent wave of immigration from Mexico, Central America, Southeast Asia, the Middle East.

Alaska

History: Settled by Russians in 1784 for fur trading. Fur animals became scarce. In

1824–25, Russia signed treaties with the United States and Great Britain. In the 1850s, Russia sold Alaska to the United States for 2 cents an acre. In 1896, a gold rush brought settlers to Alaska looking for gold. Became the 49th state in 1959.

Economy: Military bases, tourists, mining, forests, fish, animals, oil. New oil discoveries and the building of the Alaska oil pipeline brought a new economic boom.

Geography: Volcanic mountains, interior plains. Only 51 miles from the U.S.S.R. across the Bering Strait.

Climate: The Japan Current in the eastern areas of the state keeps weather mild. Cold in other parts.

People: Natives include Eskimos, Indians, and Aleuts. Migration from other U.S. states. Although it is one-fifth the size of the rest of the United States, it contains fewer people than any other state.

Hawaii

History: Polynesian voyagers reached the Hawaiian Islands as early as 800 A.D. and over the next five centuries created a society. The British captain James Cook arrived in Hawaii in 1778. U.S. missionaries and businesspeople followed, and in 1898 Hawaii became a U.S. possession. 1900: became U.S. territory. 1959: became 50th state. Hawaii asked for statehood several times; Congress was initially concerned about the loyalty of the Oriental population on Hawaii, which was proved during World War II and the Korean conflict.

Economy: Military bases, tourism, manufacturing of food products such as pineapples and sugar.

Geography: 132 islands; 8 main islands. Eighty percent of the people live on Oahu. Active and inactive volcanoes.

Climate: Warm and mild. Over 300 inches of rain a year in the mountains.

People: Original settlers were Polynesians. Christian missionaries came in the 1820s. Japanese, Chinese, Filipino, and Korean workers came later to work on pineapple and sugar cane plantations. Current population: 15 percent of Polynesian ancestry (part or full); 40 percent European (mostly from United States); 30 percent Japanese ancestry.

ASKING QUESTIONS ABOUT FAMOUS NORTH AMERICANS

You are going to play a game involving famous North Americans.

1. Look at the list of names that follows. As a class, try to think of other famous North Americans. Your instructor will write them on the board.

2. Find a partner. Choose a name from the list that follows or from the list on the board.

3. Tape the paper on your partner's back. Your partner will tape a name on your back.

4. Walk around the classroom. Ask each student one question to try to find out whose name is on your back. Ask only yes/no questions.

   Examples: Is it a man?
   Is she alive?
   Was he a politician?

5. Do not ask directly who it is. For example, you may not ask "Who is it?" or "Is it Golda Meir?"

6. Ask only one question of each person.

7. When other students ask you questions, you must answer truthfully.

Famous North Americans

George Washington	Jane Fonda	Linda Evans
Franklin D. Roosevelt	John Wayne	Martin Luther King, Jr.
Pierre Trudeau	Marilyn Monroe	Susan B. Anthony
Abraham Lincoln	Davy Crockett	Charlie Chaplin
John F. Kennedy	Golda Meir	Katherine Hepburn
Margaret Mead	Elvis Presley	Ronald Reagan
Michael Jackson	Thomas Edison	Walt Disney
Mohammad Ali	Benjamin Spock	

FINDING OUT ABOUT REGIONAL CUSTOMS IN THE UNITED STATES

You are going to ask and answer questions about four people who live in different areas of the United States.

1. Work in pairs. Sit facing each other.

2. Student 1 should look at the first chart. Student 2 should look at the second chart. Information missing on one chart is on the other, and vice versa.

3. Take turns asking each other questions to fill in the chart.

   Example: Where does Marvin live?

	Marvin	Sally Jo	Rocky	Bertha
lives		Savannah, Georgia		Des Moines, Iowa
eats for breakfast	hash brown potatoes	grits and red-eye gravy		
works			as a movie director	on her farm
favorite music	oldies: Rolling Stones, Moody Blues			Barry Manilow
favorite t.v. shows		"Hee-Haw," "Dukes of Hazzard"	never watches	
weekend activities		going on hay rides		meeting friends at the Dairy Queen
likes to visit		the Atlantic Ocean	Disneyland	
hobbies, sports	cocktail parties, basketball	swimming, playing guitar, watching football		
celebrates New Year's Day			watching the Rosebowl parade	entertaining friends at an open house or buffet

	Marvin	**Sally Jo**	**Rocky**	**Bertha**
lives	New York City		Pasadena, California	
eats for breakfast			avocados and bean sprouts	bacon, fresh eggs, coffee with cream
works	on the stock exchange	as a chicken plucker at the poultry farm		
favorite music		country: Willie Nelson and Loretta Lynn	The Grateful Dead	
favorite t.v. shows	"Miami Vice"			"Wheel of Fortune"
weekend activities	standing in line for movies		roller skating on the pier	
likes to visit	Coney Island Beach			Chicago to shop
hobbies, sports			tennis, jogging, racquetball	bowling, horseback riding
celebrates New Year's Day	recovering from a hangover	eating hog jowls and black-eyed peas		

Follow-up

Discuss the following questions with your instructor and classmates.

1. What cultural differences do you know of that exist in different regions of the United States? Think of food, celebration of holidays, speech, expressions people use, and so forth.

2. Are there regional differences in the culture of your country? Tell the class about a few of these differences. How did they begin?

8
TASTES AND PREFERENCES

EXPRESSING PREFERENCES IN MOVIES

You are going to discuss your movie preferences with a classmate.

1. Find a partner. Ask him or her the questions that follow. Write down the answers in the spaces marked "a."

2. After the interview, report one or two interesting things your found out to the class.

3. For homework, interview someone from the city you live in using the same questions. Write down the answers in the spaces marked "b."

4. Report to the class on your findings. How were the answers different from your fellow students'?

Questions

1. How many movies do you see in a week? A month?

   a. _____

   b. _____

2. What is your age? Are you male or female? Single or married?

   a. _____

   b. _____

3. What area of town do you live in? When you go to a movie, do you generally choose a theater close to home or do you drive to another area of town?

   a. _____

   b. _____

4. What's your favorite movie theater? What do you like about it?

   a. _____

   b. _____

5. How many movies have you seen in the past three months?

   a. _____

   b. _____

6. Do you generally go to movies during the week (Monday to Friday), on weekend afternoons, or on Friday or Saturday night?

   a. _____

   b. _____

7. What kind of movies do you go to see (comedy, science fiction, drama, etc.)?

   a. _____

   b. _____

8. What's the best movie you've seen this year? The worst?

   a. _____

   b. _____

9. In general, what do you think about the refreshments available in movie theaters?

   a. _____

   b. _____

10. Do movie reviews influence your movie selection at all?

    a. _____

    b. _____

Source: The Atlanta Journal/Constitution, Friday, July 27, 1984, p. 3–P.

EXPRESSING TASTES

You are going to ask a classmate questions about his or her tastes, using "What's your favorite?" or "Who's your favorite?"

1. Write your instructor's name in the space marked "Instructor's Name" in the chart on the next page.

2. Take turns asking your instructor questions using the words on the left side of the chart. For example, "What is your favorite movie?" or "Who is your favorite movie actor?"

3. Write short answers to the questions.

4. Interview a classmate. Write his or her name in the first space marked "Classmate's Name." Ask questions and write short answers. Your classmate and partner will ask you questions too. Work as quickly as possible.

5. Interview two other students if there is time. When you have finished, share some of the interesting things you've learned about your classmates.

Suggested time limits:
   First round of interviews: 8 minutes
   Second and third rounds: 5 minutes each

What/Who is your favorite . . .	Instructor's Name	Classmate's Name	Classmate's Name	Classmate's Name
movie				
movie actor				
movie actress				
food				
color				
book				
season				
sport				
vacation				

COMPARING RESTAURANTS

Do you like to sit over dinner for a long time, eating course after course, then slowly sipping coffee? Or would you rather eat someplace inexpensive where the service is fast? Or does it depend on what you're doing and how you feel? There are a wide variety of eating places to suit everyone's tastes, and in this activity you will compare some of them.

1. Choose one of the following categories of restaurants:

   cafeteria   outdoor stand
   hamburger place   24-hour coffee shop and breakfast place
   pizza place   shopping center sandwich place
   taco place   small Chinese restaurant
   large restaurant

2. Find the name and location of a restaurant in the category you chose. You can look in the phone book or ask people in your area.

3. Visit the restaurant you selected. You may go alone, in pairs, or in small groups.

4. Complete the questionnaire that follows about the restaurant you visit.

Questionnaire

1. Do you have to carry your own food to the table? (Circle yes or no.)

   yes   no

2. How long does it take to get your food? _____

3. Are the prices of the main dishes:

   _____ a. very inexpensive ($1–3)

   _____ b. inexpensive ($3–6)

   _____ c. moderate ($6–10)

   _____ d. expensive ($10 and over)

4. Can you order beer or wine in this restaurant? _____

5. Does the restaurant take credit cards? If so, which ones? _____

   _____

6. What is your overall opinion of the food, service, and atmosphere?

   _____

   _____

   _____

_____

_____

_____

Follow-up

Form a group with other people in your class who visited the same kind of restaurant that you visited.

1. List three advantages of the kind of restaurant you visited:

_____

_____

_____

2. List three disadvantages of the kind of restaurant you visited:

_____

_____

_____

3. Now discuss your results with people who visited different kinds of restaurants. Who was the most satisfied with the experience?

EXPRESSING PREFERENCES IN ART

You are going to look at some works of art and compare them.

1. Look at the works of art on the next pages.

2. Look at the questions that follow. Write your answers to the questions. Do this individually.

3. Form groups of three to five students. Compare and discuss your answers. Reach a consensus, or group agreement, on Questions 1–5.

4. Share your group's consensus with the other groups in the class. How different were the groups' opinions?

5. Which work of art was liked the best by the most people? The least? Which would the most people like to have in their home?

Virgin and Child (with Bird), French, first half of fourteenth century.

Portrait of Mrs. Alexander Allan and Daughter Matilda, Sir Henry Raeburn, England, eighteenth century.

Lady and Party with a Falcon, Nurpur, eighteenth century.

Questionnaire

1. Which work or art has the most detail? _____

2. Which is the most realistic? _____

3. Which is the most abstract? _____

4. Which do you think could be a religious work of art?

_____

5. Which is most similar to art in your country? _____

6. Which do you like best? Why?

_____

_____

Beauty on Awakening, Katsushika Tatsu Tatsujo, Japan, nineteenth century.

7. Which do you like least? Why?

_____

_____

8. Which would you like to have in your home? Explain.

_____

_____

_____

DESCRIBING REACTIONS

You are going to interview some of your classmates to find out how they feel about various things.

1. Ask your classmates questions using the words on the left of the chart below.

   Examples: What is something you're disappointed with?
   What have you been pleased with since you came to this country?

2. Take brief notes on each classmate's answers in the spaces provided. Your instructor may ask you to report some of the answers to the class.

	(name)	(name)	(name)
disappointed with/in			
bored with			
pleased with			
satisfied with			
unhappy about/with			
interested in			
surprised about/at			
excited about			

	_____ (name)	_____ (name)	_____ (name)
in favor of			
embarrassed by			
tired of			
accustomed to			

9
THE SKY ABOVE US

DESIGNING A SPACE COLONY

Imagine it is three hundred years from now and you are living in a colony in outer space. What would life be like?

1. Divide into groups of three to five students each.

2. Read the questions that follow. Discuss each one and write a group answer to it.

3. After writing answers for each category, prepare to make an oral presentation to the class about your space colony. Each person in the group should give part of the presentation. You might want to prepare a large poster showing what your space colony would look like.

Space Colony

What is the name of the colony? _____

How many people live there? _____

How large is it in area? _____

Living quarters:

What kind of rooms do you live and work in? _____

_____

What shape(s) are they? _____

What is the furniture like? _____

_____

_____

Clothing:

What do the clothes look like? _____

_____

What are they made of? _____

Food:

How do you get food? _____

Where do you get it? _____

What do you eat? _____

_____

Water:

How and from where do you get water? _____

_____

Methods of transportation:

What kinds of vehicles are there? _____

How fast do they go? _____

What do they look like? _____

_____

Daily routines:

What is the average daily routine on the space colony? _____

_____

_____

Jobs:

What kinds of jobs are there? _____

_____

_____

Social relationships:

Does marriage exist? _____

How are living units organized—for example, do people live in families?

_____

_____

Entertainment:

What do people do for relaxation, amusement, and entertainment? _____

_____

_____

_____

TELLING HOW SOMETHING IS MADE

You are going to describe how a familiar product is made.

1. Work in groups of four students.
2. Read the following paragraph, "How Is Chewing Gum Made?" Complete it with the correct forms of the verbs in parentheses (active or passive voice).
3. Read the list of products that follows the paragraph on chewing gum. Each group should choose one of the products.

4. Read the information about the product you chose. In your group, practice putting the information into sentences. Use the passive voice where appropriate.

5. Find a partner from another group. Exchange information about the products. You will have fifteen minutes for this.

6. Continue meeting with members of the other groups until you have heard about all the products.

How Is Chewing Gum Made?

An insoluble, rubberlike gum base is the main ingredient of chewing gum. At one time a rubbery material called *chicle* _____ (use). Chicle _____ (make) by boiling down the milky juice of the sapodilla tree. During the mid-1900s, synthetic gum bases that resemble chicle _____ (discover). These gum bases _____ (make) of synthetic rubber, waxes, a plastic substance called *vinyl resin*, and other types of plastics. Sometimes synthetic gum bases _____ (mix) with chicle and other natural gums.

The manufacturing process _____ (start) by melting the gum base in kettles and then pouring the soft, warm material through strainers for purification. Flavoring and sweeteners _____ (mix) in along with softeners that help the gum retain moisture. The blended gum _____ (roll) into thin, flat sheets and _____ (allow) to cool and harden. Machines then _____ (cut) the gum and _____ (break) it into individual sticks.

Products

Cigarettes

Raw materials: tobacco leaves, paper
Processing: Dry tobacco leaves and shred them into tiny pieces.
       Cut paper.
       Roll tobacco in paper.
Packaging: Put twenty cigarettes into pack or box.
       Put ten packs into a carton.
Distribution: Send by truck to grocery stores, drug stores, vending machines.

Chocolate bars

Raw materials: cocoa beans, sugar, milk, nuts
Processing: Roast cocoa beans, grind them into a powder, and blend them with sugar and milk.
       Heat.

Put nuts in rectangular molds.
Pour chocolate into molds.
Cool.
Packaging: Wrap bars in waxed paper.
Wrap with outside label.
Distribution: Send by truck to grocery stores, drug stores.

Potato chips

Raw Materials: potatoes, oil, salt
Processing: Peel potatoes and slice them thinly.
Heat oil to 500° and fry potatoes.
Drain potatoes and sprinkle them with salt.
Packaging: Seal in air-tight plastic bags.
Pack bags in cartons.
Distribution: Send to grocery stores, restaurants.

Paper bags

Raw materials: wood, chemicals, water, glue
Processing: Cut down trees, and send them to paper mill.
Chop wood into pulp and mix pulp with chemicals and water.
Roll into big sheets and dry.
Cut out sides and bottoms of bags.
Glue sides and bottoms to form bags.
Packaging: Pack into cartons.
Distribution: Send by truck to grocery stores.

T-Shirts

Raw materials: cotton, dye
Processing: Spin cotton into thread.
Machine-knit thread into lengths of cloth.
Cut out pattern.
Sew with cotton thread.
Dye with desired color.
Packaging: Pack into cartons.
Distribution: Send by truck to department stores.

Drinking glasses

Raw materials: silica sand, potash (an alkali)
Processing: Mix the silica sand and potash.
Heat to 2800°F and cook for hours to purify.
Blow or mold into shape.
Cool slowly.
Packaging: Put eight matching glasses into carton with dividers.
Distribution: Send to department stores, kitchenware stores.

LEARNING HOW TO USE THE LIBRARY: PREPARATION FOR RESEARCH

In the next activity in this chapter, you will need to know how to use the library. This is a short activity to prepare you for library reseach.

1. Sit in a circle with your classmates. Your instructor will sit outside the circle.

2. Discuss what you think are the correct answers to the questions that follow. Your instructor will listen as you discuss them.

3. After you have discussed your ideas about each question, your instructor will tell you his or her answers. As your instructor gives the answers, take notes in the spaces that follow each question.

Questions

1. What is a *card catalogue?* _____

  _____

2. How can you find a book in a library? _____

  _____

  _____

3. How do you check out a book? _____

  _____

  _____

4. How long can you usually keep a book? _____

5. How are the books organized? _____

  _____

6. What is the *Reader's Guide to Periodical Literature?* _____

  _____

7. How can you find an article on a certain topic? _____

  _____

8. What can you find in a periodicals room? _____

  _____

9. What is a *reference room?* What can you find there? _____

  _____

GIVING A SPEECH

Now that you know how to use a library, you are going to use the resources of a local library to prepare a formal, ten-minute speech. Following these directions will help you give a well-organized and interesting speech.

1. *Choosing a topic.* You should always choose a topic that will be interesting to your audience. For this speech, you may choose one of the following topics, or any topic related to the chapter theme, "The Sky above Us." Here are some suggestions:
   a. black holes
   b. Saturn: reports from Voyager I
   c. the effects of a full moon on people and animals
   d. whether or not astronauts from other planets visited earth a long time ago
   e. life on other planets or in other solar systems or galaxies
   f. an invention related to astronomy, such as the telescope
   g. early astronomers (such as Copernicus or Galileo); early beliefs about the stars and planets
   h. a recent discovery in astronomy
   i. UFOs (*unidentified flying objects*, like "flying saucers")
   j. a space exploration voyage (*Sputnik, Apollo,* or *Voyager* trips, for example)

2. *Doing your research.* Go to your local library. Look in the *Reader's Guide to Periodical Literature* under your topic and find an article to read. As you read the article, take notes on the main points only. You may need to read more than one article if the first one you choose does not have enough information.

3. *Organizing your speech.* Your speech should be organized with a clear introduction of your topic, a body of information from the article(s) you read as well as your own opinion(s), and a conclusion that sums up the speech and perhaps gives a prediction or recommendation for the future. Organize your notes for the speech in the following spaces:

   I. Introduction

II. Body

III. Conclusion

4. *Making note cards.* Transfer your notes for the speech to 3″×5″ notecards. It's better to use these than regular (8½″ × 11″) sheets of paper because they are smaller and less conspicuous and they make less noise when you move them around during the speech. You should write only brief notes to remind yourself what to say next. Do not write your speech out in complete sentences.

5. *Practicing your speech.* Give the speech to a friend or say it aloud in front of a mirror at least one time. Make sure it takes about ten minutes. Also, make sure you know how to pronounce all the words you want to use. Your instructor may give you time to practice with a partner.

6. *Giving the speech.* Here are some guidelines for giving your speech:
   a. Speak loudly and clearly so that everyone in the room can hear you.

Speech Evaluation

Names:

1. Was the speech well organized?

2. Was there enough information to make it interesting?

3. Did the speaker speak clearly?

4. Did the speaker speak naturally without reading?

5. Did the speaker make eye contact with the audience?

6. Was there a clear introduction and conclusion?

7. Did the speaker give examples and explanations of main points?

b. Look at your audience. Look at different people as you speak, not at the same one(s).

c. Vary your intonation (the level or pitch of your voice) to make your speech interesting.

d. Do not read the speech! Use your notes only as reminders. A speech is much more interesting if you speak in a natural way.

e. Try not to move your feet or your hands too much. Use your hands for natural gestures, but try to control nervous, repetitive movements.

f. Don't start with "I'm going to talk about . . . " and don't end with "Well, that's all I have to say."

g. Use visual aids if possible. A picture, chart, or map helps to focus the audience's attention and makes a speech more interesting. If you need to draw something on the board, arrange with your instructor to do it before the speech.

h. When you finish, ask for questions or comments.

7. *Evaluating the speeches.* As you listen to the other students in the class give their speeches, evaluate them using the "Speech Evaluation" form on page 90. For each question, give a rating from 1–5:

1 poor 2 fair 3 good 4 very good 5 excellent

Write the name of each speaker in the space indicated. Give your own speech an evaluation too. At the end of all the speeches, tell the class which speech you thought was best and why.

10
MEDICINE, MYTHS, AND MAGIC

TAKING A POLL: MEDICAL PRACTICES

You are going to interview some North Americans about medical practices.

1. Look at the questions in the following questionnaire. Ask a North American each question and take notes on his or her answers in the spaces provided. Then interview two more North Americans and take notes on their answers.

2. After the inteviews, share the information with the rest of the class. Then do the Follow-up exercise.

Questionnaire

	1	2	3
1. Do you have health insurance?			
2. Do you have a yearly physical checkup?			
3. How often do you go to the doctor?			
4. Have you ever been in the hospital?			
5. If yes, how would you rate the treatment (poor/fair/good/very good/excellent)?			
6. Do your doctors take time to explain things to you?			
7. Do you feel free to ask your doctor(s) any questions you have?			
8. What do you do when you have the following: a cold			
fever			
a headache			
nausea			

Questionnaire

	1	2	3
9. Did your mother use any kind of home remedies? What were they?			

Follow-up

With your classmates and instructor, answer the following questions about the questionnaire results.

1. On which question was there the greatest similarity among all the responses?

2. On which question was there the greatest difference among all the responses?

3. What percentage of the people interviewed:
   a. have health insurance?
   b. have a yearly physical checkup?
   c. have ever been in the hospital?
   d. rate their hospital treatment *very good* or *excellent?*
   e. feel free to ask their doctors questions?

4. How do you and members of your class treat simple ailments (colds, fever, headache, and nausea) differently from the people you interviewed?

5. What was the most interesting home remedy you heard about?

DETERMINING YOUR "HEALTHSTYLE": A SELF-TEST

You are going to fill out a questionnaire about your health habits and think a bit about how you could improve your health.

1. Complete the following questionnaire, "Healthstyle." Read each statement carefully and circle the number that corresponds to your health habits (*Almost Always, Sometimes,* or *Almost Never*).

2. Calculate your scores. Look at the box, "What Your Scores Mean to You." Read the information to find out what your scores mean.

3. Form groups of three to five students. Find out who has the highest scores in your group and who has the lowest. Discuss with your group members which health area you would like to change and how you would change it. Share the results of the discussion with the rest of the class.

Healthstyle: A Self-Test

All of us want good health. But many of us do not know how to be as healthy as possible. Health experts now describe *lifestyle* as one of the most important factors affecting health. In fact, it is estimated that as many as seven of the ten leading causes of death could be reduced through common-sense changes in lifestyle. That's what this brief test, developed by the Public Health Service, is all about.

	Almost Always	Some-times	Almost Never
Cigarette Smoking			
If you *never* smoke, enter a score of 10 for this section and go to the next section on *Alcohol and Drugs*.			
1. I avoid smoking cigarettes.	2	1	0
2. I smoke only low tar and nicotine cigarettes or I smoke a pipe or cigars.	2	1	0
Smoking score: _____			
Alcohol and Drugs			
1. I avoid drinking alcoholic beverages or I drink no more than 1 or 2 drinks a day.	4	1	0
2. I avoid using alcohol or other drugs (especially illegal drugs) as a way of handling stressful situations or the problems in my life.	2	1	0
3. I am careful not to drink alcohol when taking certain medicines (for example, medicine for sleeping, pain, colds, and allergies) or when pregnant.	2	1	0
4. I read and follow the label directions when using prescribed and over-the-counter drugs.	2	1	0
Alcohol and Drugs score: _____			
Eating Habits			
1. I eat a variety of foods each day, such as fruits and vegetables, whole grain breads and cereals, lean meats, dairy products, dried peas and beans, and nuts and seeds.	4	1	0
2. I limit the amount of fat, saturated fat, and cholesterol I eat (including fat on meats, eggs, butter, cream, shortenings, and organ meats such as liver).	2	1	0

	Almost Always	Some-times	Almost Never
3. I limit the amount of salt I eat by cooking with only small amounts, not adding salt at the table, and avoiding salty snacks.	2	1	0
4. I avoid eating too much sugar (especially frequent snacks of sticky candy or soft drinks).	2	1	0

Eating Habits score: _____

Exercise/Fitness

	Almost Always	Some-times	Almost Never
1. I maintain a desired weight, avoiding overweight and underweight.	3	1	0
2. I do vigorous exercise for 15–30 minutes at least 3 times a week (examples include running, swimming, brisk walking).	3	1	0
3. I do exercises that enhance my muscle tone for 15–20 minutes at least 3 times a week (examples include yoga and calisthenics).	2	1	0
4. I use part of my leisure time participating in individual, family, or team activities that increase my level of fitness (such as gardening, bowling, golf, and baseball).	2	1	0

Exercise/Fitness score: _____

Stress Control

	Almost Always	Some-times	Almost Never
1. I have a job or do other work that I enjoy.	2	1	0
2. I find it easy to relax and express my feelings.	2	1	0
3. I recognize early, and prepare for, events or situations likely to be stressful for me.	2	1	0
4. I have close friends, relatives, or others whom I can talk to about personal matters and call on for help when needed.	2	1	0
5. I participate in group activities (such as church and community organizations) or hobbies that I enjoy.	2	1	0

Stress Control score: _____

Safety

	Almost Always	Some-times	Almost Never
1. I wear a seat belt while riding in a car.	2	1	0
2. I avoid driving while under the influence of alcohol or other drugs.	2	1	0

	Almost Always	Some- times	Almost Never
3. I obey traffic rules and the speed limit when driving.	2	1	0
4. I am careful when using potentially harmful products or sub- stances (such as household cleaners, poisons, and electrical devices).	2	1	0
5. I avoid smoking in bed.	2	1	0
Safety score: _____			

What Your Scores Mean to You

Scores of 9 and 10
Excellent! Your answers show that you are aware of the importance of this area to your health. More important, you are putting your knowledge to work for you by practicing good health habits. As long as you continue to do so, this area should not pose a serious health risk. It's likely that you are setting a good example for your family and friends to follow.

Scores of 6 to 8
Your health practices in this area are good, but there is room for improvement. Look again at the items you answered with a "Sometimes" or "Almost Never." What changes can you make to improve your score? Even a small change can often help you achieve better health.

Scores of 3 to 5
Your health risks are showing! Would you like more information about the risks you are facing and about why it is important for you to change these behaviors? Perhaps you need help in deciding how to successfully make the changes you desire. In either case, help is available.

Scores of 0 to 2
Obviously, you were concerned enough about your health to take the test, but your answers show that you may be taking serious and unnecessary risks with your health. Perhaps you are not aware of the risks and what to do about them. You can easily get the information and help you need to improve, if you wish. The next step is up to you.

There's help available: In addition to personal actions you can take on your own, there are community programs and groups (such as the YMCA or the local chapter of the American Heart Association) that can assist you and your family to make the changes you want to make. If you want to know more about these groups or about health risks, contact your local health department or the National Health Information Clearinghouse, P.O. Box 1133, Washington, D.C. 20013.

ROLE-PLAYING A HEALTH PROBLEM: WHO DO YOU TRUST?

You are going to role-play a situation in which a person who is ill asks others for advice.

1. Work in groups of five. In each group, one person will take the part of the patient. The other four students in the group should each take one of the other roles.

2. Read your role carefully. If there is anything you don't understand, ask your instructor about it. Don't read the other roles. You will have twenty minutes for this role-play.

3. After the role-play, each patient should tell whose advice he or she has decided to follow and why.

4. Discuss the following question as a class: In your family, what did you do for minor illnesses such as colds, upset stomachs, fever, muscle injuries, and so forth?

Roles

1. *Patient:* You have the flu. You have a fever, and you are sneezing and coughing. You are very uncomfortable. You are going to ask four people for advice: a doctor, a pharmacist, a health-food store owner, and your mother. They will all give you different advice.

2. *Doctor:* A patient comes to you with the flu. You think it's ridiculous for someone who has only a common flu to see a doctor and take up his or her time. You are very busy and don't want to spend much time with this patient. You prescribe rest, drinking a lot of liquids (water and fruit juice), and taking aspirin.

3. *Pharmacist:* Someone comes to your store with the flu. You tell him or her that there is no cure for the flu, but you can help him or her feel more comfortable. Recommend some twelve-hour cold tablets for the sneezing, some cough medicine, and nose drops.

4. *Health-food store owner:* Someone comes to your store complaining of flu symptoms: fever, sneezing, and coughing. You don't believe in using drugstore medicines because they contain chemicals and other unnatural substances that can be harmful. You recommend lots of vitamin C and herbal teas for the fever.

5. *Mother:* Your son or daughter has the flu. You have always used the same remedies for colds and the flu: wrapping up warmly to sweat out the fever and eating lots of chicken soup. You think you read somewhere that there is scientific evidence of substances in chicken soup that fight viruses and that the steam from hot soup helps to clear up the nasal congestion and make breathing easier.

DISCUSSING FOLK BELIEFS AND SUPERSTITIONS

You are going to look at some folk beliefs and superstitions and discuss them as a class. You will also share some common folk beliefs from your culture.

1. Look at the list of beliefs and superstitions that follows. In the first box (1), put a check by those that you believe. In the second box (2), put a check by those that someone from your culture might believe.

2. What beliefs and superstitions do you know about that are not on the list? Add them in the spaces provided.

	Check (✔) those you believe.	Check (✔) those some people from your culture might believe.
1. Friday the 13th is an unlucky day.		
2. Thirteen (13) is an unlucky number.		
3. Friday the 17th is an unlucky day.		
4. Seventeen (17) is an unlucky number.		
5. Breaking a mirror brings seven years of bad luck.		
6. A black cat crossing your path can bring bad luck.		
7. Walking under a ladder can bring bad luck.		
8. Complimenting someone can bring bad luck (or can bring the "evil eye") to that person.		
9. An eclipse can bring bad luck to the unborn.		

	Check (✔) those you believe.	Check (✔) those some people from your culture might believe.
10. A full moon affects the way people behave.		
11. Carrying or wearing a particular symbol or ornament can bring good luck or can keep away the "evil eye".		
12. A demon or bad spirit lives in the ocean.		
13. Throwing salt over your right shoulder can prevent bad luck.		
14.		
15.		
16.		
17.		

Follow-up

Discuss the following questions with your instructor and classmates.

1. Of those beliefs on the list, which is believed by the most students in the class? Which is believed by the fewest students in the class?

2. Which beliefs/superstitions did you add to the list? Describe them to the class.

3. Of those you did not check, are there any you avoid anyway, just to "play it safe"? For example, would you avoid a black cat or walking under a ladder, even though you don't really believe they bring bad luck?

4. How do people in your culture express their beliefs in superstitions? For example, in countries where people believe 13 is an unlucky number, the thirteenth floor of a building is usually labeled 14, so that no floor is labeled 13. What do people in your culture *do* because of superstitions?

11
THE MEDIA

ADVERTISING: DECIDING WHICH MEDIA ARE APPROPRIATE

You are going to discuss which advertising media are appropriate for advertising various products and services.

	Adult magazines	Family magazines	News-papers	Television: after 10 P.M.	Television: anytime	Television: children's shows	Radio	Billboards	Buses
beer/wine									
hard liquor									
cigarettes									
guns									
violent movies									
birth-control products									
abortion clinics									
underwear									
political candidates									
coats made of animal furs									
candy									
expensive toys									
lawyers' services									
doctors' services									
dentists' services									

1. Read the list of products and services in the chart on page 102. Consider where you think it would be appropriate to advertise them. Put a check by those places where you would approve of each product or service being advertised.

2. Discuss your answers with your classmates and instructor. Explain why you think certain products or services should not be advertised in certain places or at certain times. In which cases did you and your classmates agree most strongly? In which cases did you disagree most strongly?

ANALYZING ADVERTISEMENTS

You are going to look at some ads for various products and answer some questions about them.

1. Form groups of three or four students each.

2. Look at the advertisements and read the questions that follow them. Answer each question as a group; the group must agree on the answer. Write your answers in the spaces that follow each question. There should be an answer for each of the ads (a, b, c and d).

a.

Reprinted with permission from Reebok International Ltd.

b.

Reprinted with permission from
Philip Morris Incorporated

Reprinted with permission from Comstock Foods

Questions

1. What is the product being advertised?

   a. _____

d.

Reprinted with permission from VISA USA Inc.

b. _____

c. _____

d. _____

2. Who would probably buy this product (men, women, teenagers, children)?

a. _____

b. _____

c. _____

d. _____

3. What age group would probably buy this product? (Give approximate years of age.)

a. _____

b. _____

c. _____

d. _____

4. What would be the socioeconomic status of the people who buy this? (That is, how much education would they have? And how much income would they have? Would they be wealthy? Middle-class? Poor?)

   a. _____

   b. _____

   c. _____

   d. _____

5. What quality of the product is emphasized or stressed in the ad (usefulness, low cost, luxury, beauty, durability, etc.)?

   a. _____

   b. _____

   c. _____

   d. _____

6. What is the psychological appeal of the ad (family closeness, appeal to the opposite sex, status, feeling of efficiency and competence)?

   a. _____

   b. _____

   c. _____

   d. _____

7. What words does the ad use to make its appeal?

   a. _____

   b. _____

   c. _____

   d. _____

8. What is there in the picture that shows the positive aspect of the product?

   a. _____

   b. _____

   c. _____

   d. _____

9. What is in the picture that is not directly connected to the product? What is in the picture for emotional appeal?

   a. _____

b. _____

c. _____

d. _____

10. What do your eyes focus on when you first look at this ad?

   a. _____

   b. _____

   c. _____

   d. _____

11. How does this ad appeal to you? Does it make you want to buy the product?

   a. _____

   b. _____

   c. _____

   d. _____

PLANNING AN ADVERTISING CAMPAIGN

You are going to plan an advertising campaign, taking into consideration the use of various media, such as television, magazines, newspapers, and radio.

1. Work in groups of five.

2. Each member of the group should take one of the following roles. Read your part carefully. Make sure you understand it.

3. The person who has the role of account representative will choose one of the following products to represent:
   a. a 32-inch television set with a built-in video recorder that sells for $2500
   b. a line of cosmetics (make-up and skin care for women)
   c. a fast-food restaurant
   d. blue jeans
   e. an instant camera
   f. a combination washer/dryer
   g. a new type of gasoline that gives twice as many miles per gallon as regular gasoline
   h. a cordless telephone

4. The person who has the role of account representative should interview each of the others. The others should give the information included with their roles. The ac-

count representative should then make a decision about what kind of advertising to buy. He or she should be prepared to tell the class what the decision was and what the reasons for it were.

Roles

1. *Account representative:* You work for an advertising agency. You are responsible for planning the advertising campaign for the product you chose. First, you are going to interview representatives from a television station, a weekly newsmagazine, a newspaper, and a radio station. Be sure to get the following information from each:
   a. How much does an ad cost?
   b. How many people are going to see or hear the ad?
   c. What kind of people will see or hear the ad (age, sex, economic status, and so forth)?
   You will have to make a decision about how to spend the money. You have $500,000 a month to spend. You do not have to spend it all on the same kind of ad. Before you conduct the interviews, think about the following things in relation to your product:
   a. Who is going to be buying this product?

   Sex: male   female

   Age: _____

   Socioeconomic status (income, education): _____

   _____

   b. What kind of appeal do you want to make? Is the product useful or a luxury?

   _____

   _____

   c. What qualities do you want to emphasize? _____

   _____

   d. What words will you use? _____

   _____

   e. What pictures will you use? _____

   _____

2. *Television ad representative:* Your job is to sell commercials on your television station. Here is the information about your ads:

Time of Show	Cost	Length of Ad	Audience
daytime	$30,000	30 seconds	mostly women: about 2 million
prime time (8:00–11:00 P.M.)	60,000	30 seconds	men, women, some children: 5 million

Time of Show	Cost	Length of Ad	Audience
late night	25,000	30 seconds	18 to 25-year-olds: 1½ million

3. *Magazine ad representative:* Your job is to sell ads in your company's magazines. Here is the information about your ads:

Type of magazine	Cost of Ad	Size of Ad	Audience
women's monthly	$25,000	half page	women: 6 million
weekly news	40,000	half page	men, women: 8 million
rock music magazine	30,000	half page	teenagers to 25-year-olds: 3 million

4. *Newspaper ad representative:* Your job is to sell ads in your newspaper. Here is the information about your ads:
Cost: $1,000
Size: half page
Time: one day
Circulation: 1 million
Selling point: newspaper ads are good for special sales because they can be changed each day.

5. *Radio ad representative:* Your job is to sell ads on your radio station. Here is the information about your ads:
Cost: $1,500
Length: 20 seconds
Time: 3 times in 1 day
Listeners: 50,000
Selling point: Your radio station is a pop rock, oldies station that appeals to the 25- to 40-year-old age group. This group statistically has a high income and spends a lot on luxury items.

CONDUCTING AN INFORMAL DEBATE: PUBLIC VS. COMMERCIAL TELEVISION

Public television is television that does not rely on commercial advertising for support. The stations receive their money mainly from the public and so do not have to worry about pleasing businesses that sponsor the programs on commercial television. Of course, raising money for programs is often a problem for public t.v. networks; commercial networks have much larger budgets and can do more expensive programs. You are going to engage in an informal debate on the following topic: "Should television be funded by commercial advertising?"

1. Before beginning to plan for the debate, discuss the following questions with your classmates and instructor.
   a. How many t.v. stations are there in your country? Is there more than one station? Do any of the stations show commercials?
   b. What is the reason for showing commercials on television? What is the alternative?
   c. What are some of the effects of t.v. advertising?

2. Divide into two equal groups. Group 1 thinks that television should be funded by commercial advertising. Group 2 thinks it should not.

3. In your groups, discuss and list all the possible reasons you can think of in favor of your group's position. Write them in the following spaces. You will have fifteen minutes to do this.

Reasons	**Name**
_____	_____
_____	_____
_____	_____
_____	_____
_____	_____
_____	_____
_____	_____
_____	_____
_____	_____

4. You must have at least one reason (argument) for each group member. Decide who will present each argument. Write the person's name beside the argument he or she will present.

5. Bring your chairs together for the debate. Line up like this:

Group 1 ○ ○ ○ ○ ○ ○ ○ ○ ○ ○ ○

Group 2 ○ ○ ○ ○ ○ ○ ○ ○ ○ ○ ○

6. Here is the format for the debate:
   a. A speaker from Group 1 presents his or her argument. (It may be very short—only a sentence or two.)
   b. Group 2 has approximately five minutes to respond. Anyone from Group 2 may speak during this time. Group 1 members may speak also, but only in response to Group 2.
   c. After no more than five minutes, the cycle begins again. Group 2 presents its first argument briefly. Group 1 may then respond, and Group 2 may answer Group 1. Each student should have a chance to present his or her argument. Then the class as a whole will discuss the debate.

12
PREJUDICE, TOLERANCE, AND JUSTICE

DISCUSSING THE PROBLEM OF DISCRIMINATION

You are going to discuss various types of discrimination (racial, religious, and so forth) and possible solutions to this problem.

1. In your country, are there groups of people who are racially or culturally different from the majority of the population? Try to identify one group of people in your country who face some type of discrimination. They may be in one of the following groups:
   a. guest workers
   b. illegal or undocumented aliens
   c. people born in your country but with a different cultural or national background from the majority
   d. people born in your country but with a different religion from the majority
   e. people who are racially or ethnically different from the majority
   f. political refugees
   If you believe that your country has no such problems, choose a group of people in another country that you know about.

2. Answer the questions that follow for the group that you have chosen.

3. Choose someone from the class to lead a discussion about the questions you answered. The discussion should focus on one category at a time (evidence, causes, possible solutions, best solution, and effects). Each person should first give evidence or facts about the discrimination problem he or she chose, then each person should discuss causes of the problem, and so forth. As you discuss each category, identify the similarities and differences among the groups discussed. Are the causes of discrimination the same? The solutions?

Questions

1. *Evidence:* How do you know that this group faces some sort of discrimination?

   _____

   _____

2. *Causes:* What are the causes of this situation? _____

   _____

   _____

   _____

   _____

3. *Possible solutions:* What are some possible solutions to the problems this group

   faces? _____

   _____

   _____

   _____

   _____

4. *Best solution:* Of the solutions listed under Question 3, which is the best? Why?

_____

_____

_____

5. *Effects:* What would be the effects, or result, of the solution listed under Question 4?

_____

_____

_____

_____

_____

_____

DISCUSSING PROBLEMS AROUND THE WORLD

You are going to discuss possible solutions to some of the problems people in various parts of the world must face.

1. Look at the incomplete questions that follow. Complete them by writing the name of a place (city or country or area of the world) in the first blank and a problem in the second blank. The problem can be any kind of problem that area faces: crime, hunger, unemployment, pollution of the environment, poverty, inflation, inadequate housing, lack of educational facilities or teachers, etc.

2. Sit in a circle with the rest of the class. Look at Question 1 and choose someone in the class who might actually know about the area and the problem. Ask that person Question 1. Several students should ask someone in the circle Question 1. Then do the same for Questions 2, 3, and 4.

Questions

1. What do you think should be done in _____ about the

   problem of _____?

2. What can de done in _____ in the next few years about

   _____?

3. What might happen in _____ regarding the

   _____ problem?

4. What should the government of _____ do about

_____?

GIVING A SPEECH

You are going to give a speech about a situation related to the topic of "Prejudice, Tolerance, and Justice."

1. Look in Chapter 9, pages 88–91, at instructions for giving a formal, prepared speech. Read them carefully.
2. Follow all the instructions from Chapter 9, but choose one of the following topics:
   a. the Civil Rights Movement in the American South, led by Martin Luther King, Jr.
   b. Mohandas Gandhi's theory of nonviolent resistance and the movement he led in India
   c. the system of apartheid in South Africa
   d. the caste system in India
   e. the Polisario Front, fighting for the separation of what used to be Spanish Morocco from Morocco
   f. the use of busing to achieve school integration in the United States
   g. the situation of one of the following groups:
      guest workers in Germany, France, or Switzerland
      racially mixed children in Korea (the children of Korean women and U.S. servicemen)
      Puerto Ricans in New York City
      Navaho Indians in the American Southwest
      Koreans in Japan
      Arabs in Israel
      Indians in South America (those who speak their own language, not Spanish or Portuguese)

ROLE-PLAYING AN ELECTION CAMPAIGN

You are going to pretend to be the citizens of Markin City. Markin City is holding elections this year for its representative to the national government.

1. Divide into two groups. Group A should be one-fourth of the class members. The rest of the students will be members of Group B.

2. Group A and Group B should each choose one person to be the political candidate for representative from Markin City to the national government.

3. Read the appropriate instructions that follow, for Candidate A, Candidate B, Group A, and Group B. Make sure you understand your role. If you have questions, ask your instructor.

4. Candidate A should meet with Group A for ten minutes. Candidate A should talk about his or her campaign and ask Group A to promise to give some money toward it. In the chart on page 118, "Candidate A: Money promised," write the amounts and sources of all the money promised. Under "Source," write where the money is going to come from (sale of house, money in the bank, etc.).

5. Candidate B should meet with Group B for ten minutes. Candidate B should also talk about the campaign and ask for money. Write the amounts and sources of money promised in the chart, "Candidate B: Money Promised."

6. If you are a member of Group A or Group B and deciding how to support your candidate, remember the following:
   a. You can sell your house, land, or car to get money to support your candidate. In order to sell your land, you must find someone willing to buy it.
   b. Housing is hard to find in Markin City. If you sell your house, you must move to a small apartment.
   c. There are no local car factories. If you sell your car, you must wait an entire year to buy a new one.
   d. If you sell your land, you will lose the income from the crops you grow on it.

7. Each candidate should add up the total amount of money promised. Your goal is to collect $100,000. If a candidate does not have the $100,000 promised, he or she should meet with the group again and try to convince them to give more money. This meeting may last ten minutes.

8. There can be a total of three meetings between each candidate and the respective group. The first candidate to collect $100,000 in pledges wins the election. If neither candidate gets $100,000, then each candidate should talk to the whole group (A and B combined) for five minutes. All citizens of Markin City may then vote for the candidate of their choice.

Roles

Group A (25 percent of the class)
You are all wealthy plantation owners. You are well educated, have worked very hard to be successful, and run your plantations well.
   You each have the following:
   a house worth $100,000
   a car worth $20,000
   land worth $1,000,000
   money in the bank: $5,000 (You just invested all your money in new farm equipment.)

You feel you treat your workers very well, giving them clothing that you don't need anymore and baskets of food at Christmas time.

You each have two teenage children who will be starting university studies in the next year or two. The universities are very expensive.

You are all worried about losing control of the government. You are afraid there might be a revolution. It is very important that you get Candidate A elected.

Group B (75 percent of the class)

You are all very poor. You work on the soybean plantations owned by the members of Group A.

You each have the following:
  a small house worth $20,000
  a car worth $5,000
  a small piece of farmland worth $5,000
  money in the bank: $5,000 (You have been working very hard and saving your money for many years.)
You eat mostly beans and potatoes, and you patch old clothes to wear.

You each have two small children. Most children of Group B in Markin City finish only six years of school. Then they go to work on the soybean plantations to help support the family. You would like your children to finish high school. That is why you have been saving your money.

Group B has never had a representative in the government before. You believe that some changes in the laws need to be made so that your children can have a better life than you have.

Candidate A

You represent Group A. You believe, basically, in keeping things the way they are. You approve of traditional values. However, you want to change the following things:

1. Members of Group A currently pay 25 percent of their income in taxes. You claim that most of this goes to support members of Group B who are too lazy to work. You want to reduce the taxes to 20 percent.

2. There have been some problems lately with members of Group B breaking into the houses of Group A and stealing money, television sets, and jewelry. You claim that this is why the members of Group B can afford to have cars. You want stronger laws with longer prison terms for criminals.

You must get Group A to contribute $100,000 to support your campaign. Talk to them, together and separately. Tell them what you want to change in the government. Convince them to give you money, even if it means selling their houses or cars.

Candidate B

You represent Group B. Group B has never had a representative to the government before because the people in Group B never had enough money to support a candidate. But now things are a little better for Group B, and, if they really get organized, they can support your campaign.

You want the following changes:

1. A minimum-wage law that would ensure all soybean workers twice the income they now have.

2. Government scholarships for the children of Group B to attend universities.

3. An increase in taxes for the rich from 25 percent to 30 percent. The extra money would pay for the scholarships and for guaranteed medical care for Group B.

You must get Group B to contribute $100,000 to support your campaign. Talk to them, together and separately. Tell them what you want to change. Convince them to give you the money, even if it means selling their houses or cars.

Candidate A: Money Promised

Amount	Person giving	Source
_____	_____	_____
_____	_____	_____
_____	_____	_____
_____	_____	_____
_____	_____	_____
_____	_____	_____
_____	_____	_____
_____	_____	_____
_____	_____	_____
_____	_____	_____

Candidate B: Money Promised

Amount	Person giving	Source
_____	_____	_____
_____	_____	_____
_____	_____	_____
_____	_____	_____
_____	_____	_____
_____	_____	_____
_____	_____	_____
_____	_____	_____
_____	_____	_____

INTERVIEWING A CLASSMATE
AND EXPRESSING WISHES

Everyone *wishes* they could change things about conditions in their countries and even world political and economic situations. You are going to find out what some of your classmates wish they could change.

1. Interview three of your classmates about what they wish about each of the topics in the following chart.
2. Take notes on their answers in the spaces to the right of the topics.
3. After the interviews, tell the class one wish that each of the people you talked to mentioned.

	name	name	name
the leader of your country			
the president of the United States			
the leader of the U.S.S.R.			
the economic situation in your country			
a world political problem			

APPENDIX

Analyzing the Changing Labor Force, Chapter 4

Percentage of Population Working in Industry in Fifteen Countries

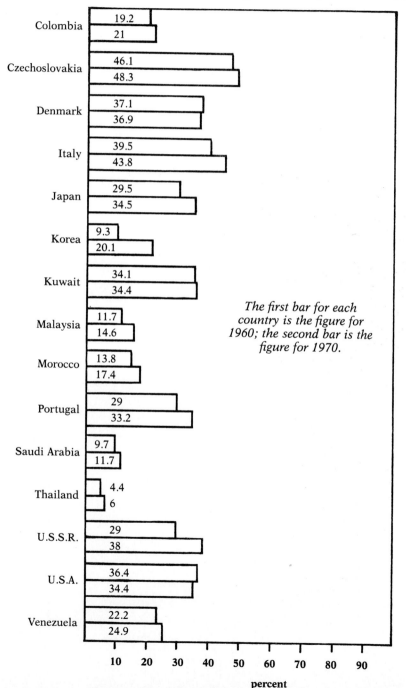

Colombia	19.2 / 21
Czechoslovakia	46.1 / 48.3
Denmark	37.1 / 36.9
Italy	39.5 / 43.8
Japan	29.5 / 34.5
Korea	9.3 / 20.1
Kuwait	34.1 / 34.4
Malaysia	11.7 / 14.6
Morocco	13.8 / 17.4
Portugal	29 / 33.2
Saudi Arabia	9.7 / 11.7
Thailand	4.4 / 6
U.S.S.R.	29 / 38
U.S.A.	36.4 / 34.4
Venezuela	22.2 / 24.9

The first bar for each country is the figure for 1960; the second bar is the figure for 1970.

10 20 30 40 50 60 70 80 90

percent

Percentage of Women Working Outside of the Home in Fifteen Countries

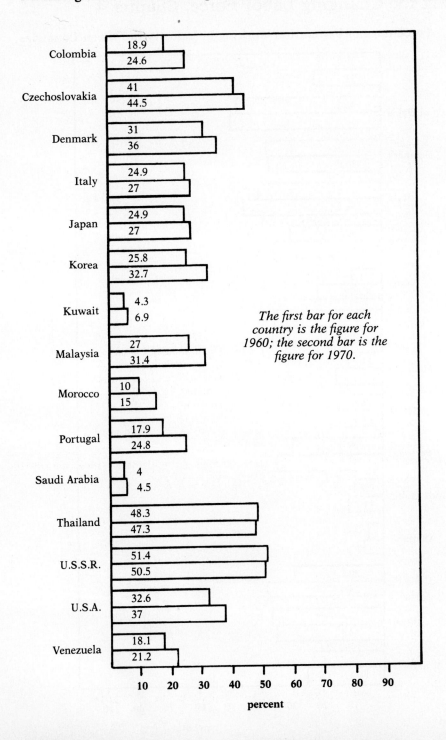

Country	1960	1970
Colombia	18.9	24.6
Czechoslovakia	41	44.5
Denmark	31	36
Italy	24.9	27
Japan	24.9	27
Korea	25.8	32.7
Kuwait	4.3	6.9
Malaysia	27	31.4
Morocco	10	15
Portugal	17.9	24.8
Saudi Arabia	4	4.5
Thailand	48.3	47.3
U.S.S.R.	51.4	50.5
U.S.A.	32.6	37
Venezuela	18.1	21.2

The first bar for each country is the figure for 1960; the second bar is the figure for 1970.

10 20 30 40 50 60 70 80 90

percent

Putting a Story in Order: Describing Marco Polo's Travels, Chapter 6

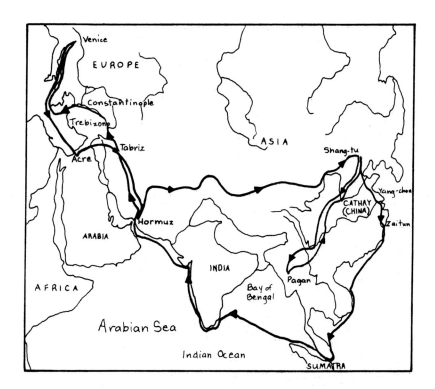

Regions of the United States, Chapter 7

Questions

1. What regions touch the Atlantic Ocean? The Pacific?

2. What regions border Canada?

3. Which areas are agricultural?

4. Which has an oil pipeline?

5. Which areas have or had oil? Gold?

6. Which area had the first college?

7. In which areas did Russian people settle? Irish? German? Dutch?

8. Which areas have had the most immigration from the Caribbean? From the Orient (Far East)?

9. Where do large numbers of American Indians live?

10. Where are there people of Polynesian ancestry?

11. Which areas are mountainous?

12. Which have volcanoes?

13. Which were the last two states of the United States?

14. Which regions have mild climates?

15. Which areas are sparsely populated?

16. Which areas produce cotton? Tobacco? Fruit? Vegetables? Salt?

17. In which areas are there factories that produce textiles? Electronic equipment? Machinery?